THE
DAILY SPARK

180 easy-to-use lessons and class activities!

THE DAILY SPARK

Critical Thinking
Journal Writing
Poetry
Pre-Algebra
SAT: English Test Prep
Shakespeare
Spelling & Grammar
U.S. History
Vocabulary
Writing

THE

DAILY SPARK

Critical Thinking

SPARK
NOTES

This edition published by Spark Publishing.

Spark Publishing
A Division of SparkNotes LLC
120 Fifth Avenue, 8th Floor
New York, NY 10011

ISBN 978-1-4114-0220-1

Please submit comments or report errors to *www.sparknotes.com/errors*.

Written by David Egan.

Printed and bound in Canada.

Introduction

The *Daily Spark* series gives teachers an easy way to transform downtime into productive time. The 180 exercises—one for each day of the school year—will take students five to ten minutes to complete and can be used at the beginning of class, in the few moments before turning to a new subject, or at the end of class. A full answer key in the back of the book provides detailed explanations of each problem.

The exercises in this book may be photocopied and handed out to the class, projected as a transparency, or even read aloud. In addition to class time use, they can be assigned as homework exercises or extra credit problems.

Critical thinking is a vital skill in any class, and the concepts covered in the *Critical Thinking Daily Spark*—logic problems, brainteasers, and more—will help students improve their overall academic performance. Mastery of these concepts will also help students succeed at writing papers and taking standardized tests.

Spark your students' interest with the *Critical Thinking Daily Spark*!

A Devious Deduction

Consider the following deduction: "Bread crumbs are better than nothing. Nothing is better than cheesecake. Therefore, bread crumbs are better than cheesecake."

What is wrong with this deduction? Do you know the name for this kind of error?

Did a Light Bulb Go Off in Your Head?

Imagine two rooms, one with three switches and the other with three light bulbs. Each switch controls one of the light bulbs. However, because the light bulbs are in a different room, you can't see immediately which switch controls which light bulb.

Your task is to figure out which switch controls which light bulb. You can spend as much time as you like in the room with the light switches, but eventually you must go into the room with the light bulbs. Once you enter the room with the light bulbs, you can't return to the room with the light switches. What's more, after entering the room with the light bulbs, you have only thirty seconds to figure out which switch controls which bulb.

How do you do it?

A Doorway to Paradise

Imagine that when you die, you will find yourself in a room with two doors, one leading to eternal paradise and the other leading to eternal damnation. You can choose which door to walk through, but the trouble is that the doors are unmarked.

Each door has a guard, and you can ask *each* guard *one* "yes" or "no" question before you make your fateful choice. One of the two guards will always answer truthfully and the other guard will always lie. Unfortunately, there's no way of knowing which guard is which.

What question should you ask one of the guards to ensure that you wind up in paradise?

Burn the Books!

The greatest library of the ancient world, which stood in Alexandria, Egypt, eventually burned down. There are many stories explaining the fire. One of them blames the seventh-century Muslim leader Caliph Omar, who reasoned that either the books in the library agreed with the Koran, in which case they were superfluous, or they contradicted the Koran, in which case they were heretical. At best the library was unnecessary, and at worst it was a danger to the faith, so Caliph Omar ordered the library burned.

This story illustrates a common error in logic. What was Caliph Omar's mistake in reasoning? Do you know the name of this mistake?

Scoring a Hat Trick

You and your two friends, Juan and Juanita, open a box with five hats in it. Three of the hats are blue, and two of the hats are yellow. The three of you close your eyes and take one hat each out of the box. With your eyes still closed, you each place the hat you're holding on your head. When you open your eyes, you see that both Juan and Juanita are wearing blue hats.

Juanita asks Juan if he knows what color his hat is. Juan says, "I don't know." Juanita replies, "Oh, then I must be wearing a blue hat."

What color is your hat?

Any Luck in Limbo?

You have stretched a piece of string around the world at the equator and have fastened it tight so that it touches the surface of the earth at every point. You cut a gap in the string and attach a second piece of string, one meter in length, so that the whole length of string is now one meter longer than it was when it was touching the surface of the earth.

Now you stretch out the string so that it is equidistant from the surface of the earth at every point. Which of the following is the closest estimate of how high the string will rise above the surface of the earth? The circumference of the earth at the equator is approximately forty million meters.

    (a) One ten-millionth of a meter
    (b) Ten centimeters
    (c) One million meters

© 2004 SparkNotes LLC

Beat the Computer

Bob claims he has invented a perfect chess computer that will win every game it plays. You play a few games against the computer, and it beats you every time. Bob takes his chess computer to the world chess championships, where it defeats every challenger. After this resounding victory, Bob proclaims that his computer is indeed perfect and will win every game it ever plays.

Do you agree with Bob? What argument might you use against him?

DAILY SPARK   CRITICAL THINKING

Get the Marble Out of the Cup

Four toothpicks have been arranged in the shape of a cup, as in the diagram below. A marble has been placed inside the cup. By moving only two toothpicks, see if you can reposition the cup so that the marble is no longer in it.

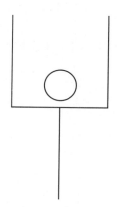

Counting on a Formula

The numbers below are arranged according to a particular formula:

1
11
21
1211
111221
312211

Can you figure out the formula? What is the next term in the sequence?

How Would You Put That Number into Words?

The following claim sounds sensible, but there is a fatal flaw in the argument. Can you identify it?

"Any number can be described in words. The number 3 can be described in a single word ('three'), while 343 can be described in five words ('three hundred and forty-three') or eight words ('the number after three hundred and forty-two') or, most economically, in two words ('seven cubed'). Because there is a finite number of words and an infinite number of numbers, there must be certain numbers that cannot be described in fewer than, say, thirteen words. And if there are certain numbers that cannot be described in fewer than thirteen words, then one of those numbers must be the smallest number that cannot be described in fewer than thirteen words."

DAILY SPARK   CRITICAL THINKING

© 2004 SparkNotes LLC

How Do 3-D Glasses Work?

3-D glasses have colored lenses: a red strip to go over the left eye and a blue strip to go over the right eye. Certain films or images have blue and red lines that appear slightly offset to the naked eye. With 3-D glasses on, however, these flat-screen images appear to be three-dimensional.

Why should wearing glasses with colored lenses make these images appear three-dimensional?

A Riddle About . . .

I am what poor people have and what rich people need. I am what blind people see and what deaf people hear. I am what brave people fear and what kind people hate. And though hateful people love me, only the biggest fools really know me.

What am I?

DAILY SPARK   CRITICAL THINKING

Connect the Dots

Nine dots are arranged in a grid, as in the diagram below.

Draw four straight lines without lifting your pencil from the paper so that the lines pass through each dot.

Water Jugs: With a Vengeance

In the film *Die Hard: With a Vengeance,* the characters played by Bruce Willis and Samuel L. Jackson have to defuse a bomb by pouring exactly four gallons of water into a jug. Their challenge is that they have only a three-gallon jug and a five-gallon jug to make their measurements with. How do they do it?

DAILY SPARK   CRITICAL THINKING

Wolves and Lambs

There are three lambs and three wolves on the left bank of a river. There is a rowboat on the left bank that can carry up to two animals at a time. All six animals want to get to the right bank of the river. However, if there are ever more wolves than lambs on either bank of the river—even if the wolves remain in the boat—the wolves will eat the lambs. The boat cannot cross the river on its own: it needs at least one animal rowing it. How can all animals get across the river without anyone being eaten?

Guessing the Hats

Ten female cadets are lined up in a column one behind the other, all facing the same direction. They are blindfolded. Their drill officer places either a red or a blue beret on each cadet's head. When the blindfolds are removed from the cadets' eyes, they can see the color of the berets of all the cadets in front of them, but cannot see the color of their own beret or of any of the berets behind them.

Starting with the cadet at the back of the line, each cadet in turn has to guess the color of her own beret. Obviously, there is no way for the first cadet to guess the color of her beret with any confidence. However, if the cadets plan carefully beforehand, they can be sure that every other cadet will be able to guess correctly.

What system can they use to be sure of making nine out of ten correct guesses?

Hint: This is a very difficult problem. If the first cadet were to say the color of the beret immediately in front of her, the second cadet would be able to guess correctly, but the third cadet would be at a loss. What can the first cadet say that will comment not just on the beret directly in front of her, but also on all the berets in front of her?

1 = 2

Early in your education, you probably learned that $1 + 1 = 2$. However, it is possible to prove that $1 = 2$. You don't need very advanced math to follow this proof. You just need a little algebra, starting with two variables, x and y, which represent the same number:

Given: $x = y$
Multiply each side by x to get: $xy = x^2$
Add x^2 to each side to get: $x^2 + xy = x^2 + x^2$
This can be rewritten as: $x^2 + xy = 2x^2$
Now subtract $2xy$ from each side to get: $x^2 + xy - 2xy = 2x^2 - 2xy$
This can be rewritten as: $x^2 - xy = 2x^2 - 2xy$
This, in turn, can be rewritten as: $1(x^2 - xy) = 2(x^2 - xy)$
Divide both sides by $x^2 - xy$ to get: $1 = 2$

Okay, just kidding. 1 does not equal 2. But can you figure out what is wrong with the proof we gave?

A Fundamental Error

"The Bible says that God exists. The Bible is also the word of God. The word of God is necessarily true. Therefore, everything in the Bible is necessarily true. So if the Bible says that God exists, then God must exist."

What is wrong with this argument? Do you know the name of the fallacy involved?

Eratosthenes in the Round

Eratosthenes of Cyrene was a Greek scholar and mathematician of the third century B.C.E. who, among other things, made a remarkably accurate estimate of the circumference of the earth.

His method involved placing a stick in the ground a few hundred miles north of the Tropic of Cancer on the summer solstice and measuring the shadow cast by the stick.

How could he estimate the circumference of the earth based on the shadow cast by this stick?

A Cretan Cretin

Epimenides the Cretan famously announced, "All Cretans are liars." Is this true?

Feathers and Gold

Which weighs more: a pound of feathers or a pound of lead?

Which weighs more: a pound of lead or a pound of gold?

Run That Race

If you are in a race and you pass the person in second place, what place will you be in?

Color the Map

Suppose you wanted to color a world map so that no two countries sharing a border had the same color. Also suppose that you wanted to use as few colors as possible. How many colors would you need?

A Multicolored Map

In the previous problem, you found that you could color any map you like with four colors and no two regions sharing a border would also share the same color. This is true of flat maps and of globes, but there are other kinds of surfaces where four colors isn't enough. Can you think of one and draw a map that would require five colors?

Hint: Think cops.

A Throw of the Dice

If you roll two dice, what number is most likely to come up?

Follow the Sequence

What is the next number in this sequence?

1, 1, 2, 3, 5, 8, . . .

Do you know the name of this type of sequence?

Drawing Socks

It's time to get up. You roll out of bed, eyes still closed, and stagger over to your sock drawer. You know that you have three green socks, five red socks, eight blue socks, nine black socks, and twelve white socks scattered at random in the drawer. How many socks will you need to withdraw (keeping your eyes closed) in order to be *sure* you've got a matching pair?

A False Cause

"*A* happened. Then *B* happened. If *A* had not happened, then *B* would not have happened either. Therefore, *A* caused *B*."

Can you think of a counterexample to prove that this reasoning is wrong?

DAILY SPARK   CRITICAL THINKING

A Family Fishing Expedition

Two fathers and their sons go fishing. Each person on the fishing trip catches a fish. In total they catch three fish. How is this possible?

Sorting out the Syllogisms

A syllogism is a three-part logical deduction. One of the simpler kinds of syllogisms, called a **categorical syllogism**; runs as follows: "All F's are G; x is an F; therefore, x is a G." "All F's are G" is called the **major premise**; "x is an F" is called the **minor premise**; and "x is a G" is called the **conclusion**.

Think of an example of a categorical syllogism for each of the following:

1. The major premise is false, but the minor premise and conclusion are both true.
2. The minor premise is false, but the major premise and conclusion are both true.
3. Both the major and minor premises are false, but the conclusion is true.

Counting with the String Clock

You have two identical pieces of string. You know that if you light one of these pieces of string at one end, it will take exactly an hour for the string to burn completely. However, neither piece of string is evenly made, so each might burn faster at one point and slower at another.

With just these two pieces of string and a lighter, how can you measure exactly 45 minutes?

A Bit of Geography

We call a country **landlocked** when it is surrounded by other countries and doesn't touch the sea or ocean at any point. We could then call a country **doubly landlocked** if it is surrounded only by other landlocked countries, and doesn't share a border with a country that touches the sea or ocean.

There are two doubly landlocked countries in the world. What are they? This is a very difficult question, so you get a few hints.

Hint 1: One of the countries is in Europe and the other is in Asia.
Hint 2: The country in Europe is very small, and the country in Asia used to be a part of the Soviet Union.
Hint 3: The country in Europe begins with an *L,* and the country in Asia begins with a *U.*

If you still need help, check a map!

DAILY SPARK CRITICAL THINKING

© 2004 SparkNotes LLC

Slanted Statistics

What is wrong with the reasoning in the following statement?

"Last Monday, my team of researchers randomly called 1,000 people at home between the hours of 11 a.m. and 3 p.m. to determine the percentage of the population that has full-time jobs. Of the people we surveyed, only 60% have full-time jobs. There is clearly a crisis of unemployment in this country."

A Long, Strange Trip

Roald plants a flag in the ground. He walks thirty miles due north, then thirty miles due west, then thirty miles due south. He finds himself back at the flag he planted. Where is he?

DAILY SPARK CRITICAL THINKING

© 2004 SparkNotes LLC

A Short, Strange Trip

Helga is on a boat in the ocean. The time is 9 p.m. on a Sunday. She starts heading due east. After traveling for 250 miles she takes a rest. The time is now 9:05 p.m. on the same Sunday. At no point was the boat traveling faster than the speed of sound. How is this possible?

Flip a Coin

You have flipped a perfectly normal coin ten times and gotten heads every time. What is the probability that you will get heads the next time you flip it?

© 2004 SparkNotes LLC

Flip and Switch

Here is a game where you try to order the digits from one to nine in as few moves as possible. Let's start with the string of numbers 382546197. In any given move, you can reverse the order of anywhere between two and nine digits, counting from the left. So, for example, if you wanted to reverse the first five digits counting from the left, you would change 382546197 into 452836197, and if you wanted to reverse the first three digits of this new string of numbers, you would get 254836197.

Try to transform 382546197 into 123456789 in as few moves as possible. What strategies can you use to improve your score?

© 2004 SparkNotes LLC

A Flat Earth Problem

You have a very stubborn friend who refuses to believe anything he's told, trusting only facts that he can observe or that are proven to him. He's been told since childhood that the earth is round, but he doesn't believe it because he's never seen any proof. What proof could you give him that the earth is round?

Mystery Number

A number gives you the following clues as to its identity:

1. I am a two-digit number
2. I am not prime
3. My two digits are not the same
4. I am not a multiple of 2, 3, or 5

What is the number?

Measuring Marbles

You have nine marbles, one of which weighs slightly more than the other eight. However, the heavier marble looks the same as the other marbles, and the difference in weight is negligible enough that you can't tell which is the heavier marble simply by holding it in your hand.

Fortunately, you have a weighing scale, which consists of two pans balanced against one another. What's the smallest number of weighings you would need to do to determine which is the heavy marble?

A Study of Suicide

What is wrong with the following argument?

"Suicide is the third leading cause of death among men in their twenties, and only the fourteenth leading cause of death among men in their seventies. Clearly, young men are far more likely to kill themselves than old men, so we should concentrate our suicide prevention efforts on young men."

A Tricky Relay

Alba, Bobo, Coco, and Dodo are in a relay race that has the following rules: two people on the team must run together from one side of a field to the other, carrying a baton, then one person on that side of the field must carry the baton back. The goal is to get all four people across the field.

Alba takes one minute to run across the field, Bobo takes two minutes, Coco takes five minutes, and Dodo takes ten minutes. When two people run together, they can only go as fast as the slower of the two runners. Alba, being the fastest, suggests that she should run across with each of the others in turn. She says this will save time because she can run back to pick up the next teammate in only one minute. A quick calculation suggests this would take the team nineteen minutes. Coco points out that there is another method they could use that would take only seventeen minutes. What method is this?

The Frozen North

Why is it generally colder closer to the poles and warmer closer to the equator?

A Quick Count

If you were to write out all the numbers from 1 to 500,000, would you have written more 2s or more 7s, or would you have written the same number of both?

Measure the Longitude

Navigators have long known the secret to measuring latitude: depending on where the sun and stars sit in the sky, you can calculate how far north or south you are. However, the problem of measuring longitude—calculating how far east or west you are—mystified scholars and navigators for centuries.

John Harrison, an eighteenth-century clock maker, solved the problem of measuring longitude by inventing the chronometer, a remarkably accurate, durable, and consistent timepiece. How could a good clock help you determine how far east or west you are?

Feeding the Family

A poor farmer is able to produce sixteen bowls of rice per day to feed his family of seven. He notices that he and his family are rather sloppy eaters, and that for every four bowls of rice eaten, he can scrape the leftovers from those four bowls to fill another bowl. Using this system, he hopes to be able to feed each family member three bowls of rice per day. Can he do it?

Improvident Proverbs

Proverbs are short, familiar sentences that are meant to help us lead better lives. Sometimes, however, proverbs seem to contradict one another. For each of the following five pairs of proverbs, explain whether you think the apparent contradiction between them can be reconciled, and if so, how.

"Absence makes the heart grow fonder" vs. "Out of sight, out of mind"
"Look before you leap" vs. "He who hesitates is lost"
"You're never too old to learn" vs. "You can't teach an old dog new tricks"
"It's better to be safe than sorry" vs. "Nothing ventured, nothing gained"
"Many hands make light work" vs. "Too many cooks spoil the broth"

Whose Son Are You?

A man and his young son get in a car accident. The man dies, and the injured son is rushed to hospital. At the hospital, a doctor operates on the boy, saving his life. The boy is the doctor's son.

How is this possible?

Circle the Dots

There are ten dots laid out in a row on this page:

•   •   •   •   •   •   •   •   •   •

Taking turns with a partner, circle either one or two dots. The object is to force your partner to be the one who circles the last dot.

Can you devise any strategies for winning this game?

The Tower of Hanoi

According to a legend invented by a nineteenth-century French mathematician, the Tower of Hanoi is a majestic temple consisting of sixty-four fragile golden disks, all of different sizes, balanced on top of one another, with the largest at the bottom. The temple priests wish to move the temple, but they can only do so by moving one disk at a time, and can never place a larger disk on top of a smaller disk. When they have completed their task, the temple will crumble into dust and the world will end in a giant clap of thunder.

They're still working at it, so we'll move on to a similar but easier puzzle. Suppose you have only four disks on a peg and you need to move them to a third peg, but you can only move one disk at a time and can never place a larger disk on a smaller one. What is the least number of moves in which you can reconstruct your four-disk tower on the third peg?

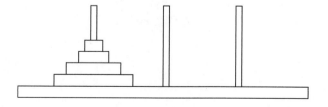

The Business of Government

What is wrong with the following argument?

"Government is like business. And just as any sensible business should worry first and foremost about the bottom line, so should any sensible government."

Separate the Particles

You have a bowl full of iron filings, sugar, and mustard seeds. You decide you want to separate the three kinds of particles. What might you do to separate the iron filings, sugar, and mustard seeds?

DAILY SPARK   CRITICAL THINKING

A Salty Solution

In freezing cold weather, people often sprinkle salt on the sidewalks and roads. How does this help?

Debating the Declaration

What is wrong with the following argument? Do you know the name of the mistake being made?

"The Declaration of Independence says that all men are created equal. But we aren't all created equal: some of us are born smarter or healthier or more athletic or bigger. So the Declaration of Independence is mistaken."

The Death of a President

What is wrong with the following argument?

"Since 1840, Ronald Reagan is the only president to have been elected in a year ending with a zero who did *not* die while still in office. Since George W. Bush was elected in 2000, there is a high probability that he will die while still in office."

Eleven Guests in Ten Beds

An hotelier runs a small hotel in which there are ten beds. One evening, eleven brothers show up at the hotel. Not wanting to turn any of them away, the hotelier comes up with a brilliant solution. He asks the first two brothers to lie in the same bed temporarily. He then puts the third brother in the second bed, the fourth brother in the third bed, the fifth brother in the fourth bed, and so on, until he puts the tenth brother in the ninth bed. That leaves the tenth bed free, so he then goes to fetch the second brother from the first bed and allows him to sleep there.

Has the hotelier succeeded in cheating logic?

Choose Your Manner of Death

While traveling in a foreign country, you inadvertently break one of that country's capital laws. You are brought before a judge who explains that you will be put to death. The law states that you have some choice in the manner of your death. You are asked to make a single statement. If that statement is true, you will be put in the electric chair. If that statement is false, you will have your head chopped off.

What can you say to avoid being executed altogether?

How Warm Is It Getting?

What is wrong with the following argument?

"Environmentalists keep warning us about global warming. But this winter was colder than the last one. This whole global warming scare is a hoax."

DAILY SPARK   CRITICAL THINKING

Vanishing Money

Three sisters go out for a meal at a restaurant. At the end of the meal, they each give the waiter ten dollars, for a total of thirty dollars. When the waiter looks at the tab, he realizes the sum only came to twenty-five dollars. He decides not to show the sisters the tab, but instead pockets two of the dollars for himself and then returns one dollar to each of the sisters, explaining that they'd paid too much.

At the end of the night, then, each of the sisters has paid nine dollars (ten minus one), and the waiter has pocketed two. Three times nine is twenty-seven, plus two is twenty-nine. But the three sisters originally paid thirty dollars. Where did the extra dollar go?

Murderous Capitals

Is the following conclusion correct?

"In Moscow, there were 1,275 murders in 2002. In Washington, D.C., there were 262 murders in 2002. Clearly, the American capital is much safer than the Russian capital."

Count Up the Snow

Sally lives on a farm that covers ten square kilometers. On Christmas Day, it snows steadily from morning till night. Sally, being a mathematically inclined farmer, decides she wants to estimate how many snowflakes fell on her farm on Christmas Day.

How might Sally go about making her estimate?

Taking Aim

There are ninety-seven birds sitting in a tree. Shotgun Sharon swaggers up to the tree and fires three whole rounds of ammunition at the birds. She kills twice as many in the first round as in the second round, and twice as many in the second round as in the third round. In the third round she kills three birds.

How many birds are left in the tree after Sharon fires off the third round?

Reading the Graph

What is wrong with the following argument?

"The graph below shows how many units of A-1 Widgets we sold at our three stores in the past month. As you can see, the performance of Store *A* was twice as strong as that of Store *B*, and Store *C*'s performance really isn't worth mentioning. I recommend that we empty our stock out of our unproductive stores and ship it all to Store *A*."

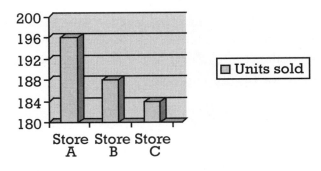

The Cost of Apples

Two farmers, Pierre and Angus, are selling their apples at a market, Pierre at the price of three for a dollar and Angus at the price of two for a dollar. At 6:30, both farmers have to leave for the opera, but each has thirty apples left to sell. Rather than miss the opera or lose their sales, they ask Ed, a friend of theirs, to sell the rest of their apples for them.

Ed decides that he'll sell all sixty apples at five for two dollars. Sales are brisk, and by the end of the day he's sold all sixty apples at the price of five for two dollars, making a total of twenty-four dollars.

Pierre and Angus return from the opera and ask for their money. Pierre, who was selling at three for a dollar, wants ten dollars for his thirty apples, and Angus, who was selling at two for a dollar, wants fifteen dollars for his thirty apples. Between the two of them, they want twenty-five dollars, but Ed only made twenty-four dollars.

What happened to the extra dollar?

The Truth About Tattoos

You are visiting an island populated by two tribes: the Eagles and the Lions. The Eagles all have eagles tattooed on the soles of their feet, while the Lions all have lions tattooed on the soles of their feet. The Eagles are known for their honesty: no Eagle has ever told a lie. The Lions are known for their dishonesty: no Lion has ever told the truth.

You are at a meeting with three natives of the island and are trying to figure out to which tribe they belong. Unfortunately, both tribes consider it very rude to show the soles of their feet to foreigners. So you ask the first islander what is tattooed on the soles of his feet. This islander understands English, but doesn't speak it, so he responds in his native tongue. You turn to the second islander and ask her what the first islander said. She tells you, "He said he has eagles tattooed on his feet." Not sure if you should trust her, you ask the third islander what the second islander has on her feet. The third islander answers, "She has lions tattooed on her feet."

What does the third islander have on his feet?

Pushing the Envelope

Below is a picture of an open envelope. See if you can reproduce this picture without lifting your pencil from the page and without retracing any lines.

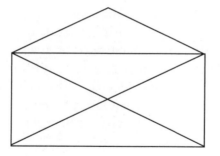

DAILY SPARK   CRITICAL THINKING

An Empty Riddle

The more you take away from me, the bigger I become. What am I?

The Execution Balls

You have been given a death sentence in a foreign country. The night before your execution, you are brought two boxes, one containing fifty red marbles and one containing fifty blue marbles. All the marbles are the same size, weight, and shape. You are told that on the following day, the executioner will be blindfolded and will put his hand into one of the boxes and remove a marble. If the marble is blue, your life will be spared. If the marble is red, you will be executed.

You can arrange the marbles in the two boxes however you like, but you can't leave out any marbles, and you can't leave either box empty. Also, the executioner is known to take his time choosing a marble, so you can't improve your chances by stacking all the blue marbles at the top.

How can you arrange the marbles in the boxes so as to maximize your chances of surviving?

Counting Out of Sequence

In each of the following sequences, one of the numbers is out of place. Identify the number that is out of place and replace it with the correct one.

1, 4, 8, 16, 25, 36

1/6, 1/3, 1/2, 2/3, 4/5, 1

2, 3, 5, 7, 10, 13, 17

A Strange House Indeed

Paolo lives in a square house that has one window on each of its sides. All four of the windows face north. How is this possible?

A Game Game

The philosopher Ludwig Wittgenstein proposed that there is no definition or set of defining characteristics for the word *game* that includes all the things we would consider a game and excludes all the things we would not consider a game.

Come up with three possible definitions for the word *game*, and for each definition provide a counterexample, either of a game that is not included under that definition or of something that is not a game that is included under that definition.

Can you come up with a definition of *game* for which you can think of no counterexamples?

Boys and Girls

In the DeWitt family, every boy has as many brothers as sisters, and every girl has twice as many brothers as sisters. How many siblings are there in the DeWitt family? How many girls are there? How many boys?

A World Without God

What is wrong with the following argument?

"All the so-called 'proofs' of God's existence that were advanced by medieval philosophers have since been proven invalid. Therefore, we can safely assume that God does not exist."

Item of Mystery

The person who makes it doesn't tell what it is.
The person who accepts it doesn't know what it is
The person who knows what it is doesn't want it.

What is it?

Hawks and Doves

What is wrong with the following reasoning? Do you know the name for this sort of fallacy?

"Jack is opposed to the war, but he's a coward. I wouldn't take any of his arguments seriously."

Outrunning the Tiger

Two explorers are walking in the jungles of India. They come to a clearing, where they see a tiger. The tiger snarls and starts to approach them. Quickly, one of the explorers digs into his pack, pulls out running shoes, and starts putting them on. The other explorer looks at him quizzically and says, "Surely you don't think you can outrun a tiger?"

"I don't think I can outrun the tiger," replies the explorer, "but these running shoes will still save my life."

How will the running shoes save him?

Dancing for Money

Accept the following three premises as true:

"All my friends are dancers."
"If no convicted criminals are dancers, then no dancers are rich."
"I have a rich friend."

Does it follow that some dancers are convicted criminals?

Ball Bearings in a Box

I have a large cardboard box with a few ball bearings in it. I put the box in a tub of water. The ball bearings weigh down the box a bit, but it still floats. I decide to take one of the ball bearings out of the box and drop the ball in the tub. Does the water level in the tub rise, fall, or remain the same as it was with the box floating on its surface?

Another Hat Trick

The Brain Olympics have come down to the medal round, with only three competitors left. For the final event, the three competitors are told that they will be blindfolded and a pink or green hat will be placed on each of their heads.

The three are blindfolded, and a green hat is placed on each person's head. When the blindfolds are removed, the competitors are told to raise their hand if they see someone wearing a green hat. Naturally, all three competitors raise their hands. The judge then announces, "The first one of you to guess the color of your own hat will win the gold medal!" All three look at each other for a couple of minutes. Then one of them excitedly announces, "I am wearing a green hat!"

How does this competitor know what color his hat is?

A SparkNotes Trilogy

You love SparkNotes so much that you decide to get each of your three favorite SparkNotes books bound with a fancy leather binding. The pages of each SparkNotes book are one inch thick, and the leather binding is one quarter of an inch thick.

When you arrange the three SparkNotes books in order on your bookshelf, what is the distance between the first page of the first book and the last page of the last book?

Moving Buttons

You have six buttons arranged on a table as diagrammed below. By moving only two buttons, arrange them so that they form one row of three buttons and one row of four buttons.

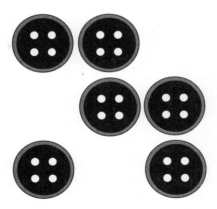

Sorting out the Sequence

What letter comes next in the sequence below?

IIIIIIVVVIVIIVIIII

DAILY SPARK   CRITICAL THINKING

Fake Gold

You have five bags containing ten gold coins each. Each coin should weigh ten grams. However, the coins in one of the bags have been minted with impurities, so that each coin weighs only nine grams.

You have a large weighing scale that will give a readout accurate to the nearest gram. How can you figure out which bag contains the lighter coins with just one readout?

Watching Guns

You are sailing on a lake. Suddenly, a mysterious stranger standing on the shore points a rifle at you and fires. Fortunately, the shot misses and the bullet enters the water right next to your boat.

In what order do you experience the following?

(a) See the splash on the water
(b) See the flash of the rifle firing
(c) Hear the gunshot

Summing the Sequence

What is the sum of the following problem? Note: The ellipses (. . .) below mean, "Continue the problem through 99. $(8 - 9 + 9 - 10$, etc)."

$1 - 2 + 3 - 4 + 5 - 6 + 7 - 8 + \ldots - 100$

Evaluating Historical Documents

The study of history relies heavily on documents. Documents can be primary sources (recorded by eyewitnesses soon after the event took place), or they can be secondary sources (recorded some time after the fact by people not directly involved). Not only written works, but photographs, artifacts, audio recordings, and so on are considered historical "documents."

For each of the following documents, list one factor that might help an historian uncover the truth, and one factor that might prevent an historian from uncovering the truth.

A photograph

An eyewitness account of an event (i.e., a description from someone who saw it happen)

A history textbook

A news broadcast given at the time of the event

DAILY SPARK • CRITICAL THINKING

Breeding Like Bacteria

At 8 a.m., you place a certain amount of bacteria on a slide. Every hour, the area covered by the bacteria doubles. By 5 p.m., the slide is covered with bacteria. The area of the slide is 2 cm².

At what time was half the slide covered with bacteria?

Shooting Down Bad Arguments

What is wrong with the following argument?

"All criminals carry guns. Jerry carries a gun. Therefore, Jerry is a criminal."

DAILY SPARK   CRITICAL THINKING

Digging Up the Past

A friend of yours returns from an archaeological dig in Italy and shows you a coin she dug up. The coin looks very old and is inscribed with the words "47 B.C." Your friend offers to sell it to you for just $20. Do you take her up on the offer?

A Horse With Nine Legs

What is wrong with the following argument? Do you know the name of the error being made?

"One horse has four more legs than no horse. No horse has five legs. Therefore, one horse has nine legs."

DAILY SPARK   CRITICAL THINKING

Another Sequence of Letters

What's the next letter in the following sequence?

O T T F F S S

Find the Missing Animal

Which of the following animals does not belong in this list, and why?

Polar bear, penguin, beluga, moose, walrus, reindeer

Threat Assessment

What is wrong with the following argument?

"Tony said he wouldn't come out if there were a hockey game on tonight. But there isn't a hockey game on, so he's bound to join us."

© 2004 SparkNotes LLC

Numbering the Regions

In the diagram below, each region has a number in it. What number should go in the region with the question mark?

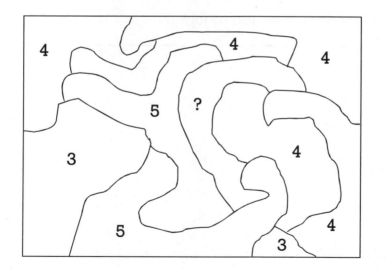

Shapes Within Shapes

Consider the following sequence of shapes:

  ?

Which of the following should fit in the space with the question mark?

An Oldie but a Goodie

As I was going to St. Ives,
I met a man with seven wives.
Every wife had seven sacks,
Every sack had seven cats,
Every cat had seven kits.
Kits, cats, sacks, wives,
How many were going to St. Ives?

DAILY SPARK   CRITICAL THINKING

Drawing the Line

You line up six friends from tallest to shortest, in order from left to right: Andy, Beatrice, Colin, Danielle, Ernie, and Florence. When you leave the room, however, the six friends decide to mix up the order they're standing in. They lock the door to the room and tell you that you can't come back in unless you can guess what order they're standing in now. They give you the following hints:

1. No one is standing in the place he or she was standing in to begin with.
2. Ernie is immediately to the right of Beatrice.
3. Neither Danielle nor Florence is standing third from the left.
4. Ernie is to the left of Andy and Colin is immediately to the right of Andy.
5. Florence is to the left of Danielle.
6. A girl is standing in the second place from the right.

In what order are they standing now?

Odd One Out

Which of the following does not belong in this list, and why?

Green pepper, oak tree, mushroom, fern, grass, rose

DAILY SPARK   CRITICAL THINKING

© 2004 SparkNotes LLC

DAILY SPARK   CRITICAL THINKING

Dividing the Herd

A farmer has seventeen cows and three sons. He dies, leaving the following will:

"My oldest son will receive one half of the cows, my second son will receive one-third of the cows, and my third son will receive one-ninth of the cows. Each son must receive exactly the proportion I have specified, and none of the cows may be cut into parts. If my sons cannot find a way to share my cows properly, then none of them deserve them, and I give my cows instead to my neighbor, who has one cow."

What can the sons do to win their inheritance?

© 2004 SparkNotes LLC

Multiplication Calculation

Without using a calculator, figure out the product of $0 \times 1 \times 2 \times 3 \times 4 \times 5 \times 6 \times 7 \times 8 \times 9$.

© 2004 SparkNotes LLC

Langford's Problem

The Scottish mathematician C. Dudley Langford invented the following problem:

It is possible to arrange two 1s that are separated by one digit, two 2s that are separated by two digits, and two 3s that are separated by three digits as follows: 3 1 2 1 3 2.

Can you do the same for four number pairs? That is, arrange two 1s that are separated by one digit, two 2s that are separated by two digits, two 3s that are separated by three digits, and two 4s that are separated by four digits?

Estimating Length

Without using a ruler, estimate which of the lines below is longer, the horizontal line or the vertical line:

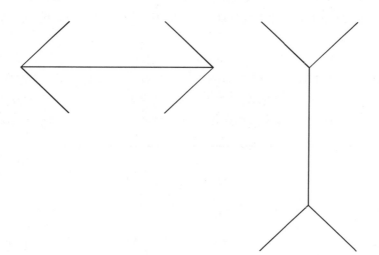

DAILY SPARK   CRITICAL THINKING

© 2004 SparkNotes LLC

Boozing and Losing

What is wrong with the following argument? Do you know the name of this kind of fallacy?

"Adults opposed to underage drinking are primarily concerned that young people shouldn't have too much fun. But young people have just as much of a right to enjoy themselves as anyone else. Therefore, the adults opposed to underage drinking are unjustified killjoys."

Deduce This

If the following premise is true, can people love themselves?

"Nobody loves someone who is loved by someone they love."

A Truckload of Birds

Your friend Bob the bird collector has decided to move his collection of one thousand bluebirds from one town to the next. To do so, he releases all the bluebirds into the back of a big box truck. At first, all of the bluebirds sit on the floor of the box truck. But as he starts to drive, the bluebirds get excited and start flying around.

Does the weight of the box truck decrease when the bluebirds start flying?

A Library of Catalogues

A certain library contains only catalogues of the titles of other books. One wing of the library contains catalogues of titles of regular books, while another wing contains catalogues of catalogues, many of which list their own titles along with the titles of other catalogues.

One catalogue contains a catalogue of all the catalogues that do not list themselves. Is this catalogue itself listed within its own pages?

Apples and Oranges

You are presented with three boxes. One contains only apples, one contains only oranges, and one contains a mix of apples and oranges. Each box has a label on it, one saying "apples," one saying "oranges," and one saying "apples and oranges"—but each one of these labels has been placed on the wrong box. You can't look into any of the boxes to see which contains what, but you can remove one fruit from one of the boxes.

What can you do to set the labels right?

© 2004 SparkNotes LLC

Thinking Inside the Box

Without drawing any lines outside the box, and without letting any two lines cross over one another, see if you can draw four lines connecting each box with the other box of the same color. The lines needn't be straight.

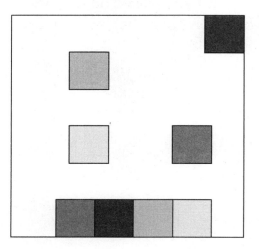

© 2004 SparkNotes LLC

DAILY SPARK   CRITICAL THINKING

Roll With It

A car tire rolls over a pebble on the road, as in the diagram below:

Which of the arrows below shows the direction in which the tire will kick the pebble?

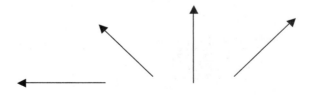

Familiar Tongues

Fractals are figures that are generated by repeating a process again and again, infinitely. One famous example is the Koch snowflake. In each iteration, you place triangles one third the size of the triangles of the previous iteration in the middle of every line. Below are the first three iterations of the process:

If you repeat this process infinitely, will the area of the resulting figure be finite or infinite? Will its perimeter be finite or infinite?

Tracing Past History

The science of genetics is very complicated and no one fully understands it, but there are some simple patterns. One example is eye color. Every person has two eye color genes. If both of these genes are for brown eyes, the person will have brown eyes. If both of these genes are for blue eyes, the person will have blue eyes. If a person has one brown eye gene and one blue eye gene, that person will have brown eyes, because brown eyes are dominant and blue eyes are recessive.

We can represent the blue eye gene with a lowercase "b" and the brown eye gene with an uppercase "B." So we would represent a person with one blue eye gene and one brown eye gene as "Bb."

Alison has four grandparents. Her mother's mother is Bb and her mother's father is bb. Her father's mother is BB and her father's father is Bb. What is the probability that Alison has blue eyes?

Find Your Family

Mr. and Mrs. Egan are having a dinner party for a number of important guests. They are serving roast duck as the main course. While Mrs. Egan entertains the guests, Mr. Egan goes into the kitchen to remove the duck from the oven. As he carries the duck in on a platter, he trips and the duck falls onto the floor.

What can Mrs. Egan say to rescue the situation, so that she and her husband will still have a meal to serve and the guests won't think they're eating a dirty duck?

Mutual Admiration

From the following two premises, can you determine whether someone you admire will also admire you?

"If you admire someone, you also admire the people whom that person admires."

"No one admires him or herself."

Euthyphro's Mistake

In Plato's dialogue *Euthyphro,* the character Euthyphro presents himself as an expert on religious matters. He claims that the gods approve of things that are holy. When asked to define what makes something holy, he says that something is holy if the gods approve of it.

What is wrong with Euthyphro's reasoning? What sort of error is this?

Climbing Up the Well

A spider falls to the bottom of a ten-foot well. The spider climbs up two feet every day, but every night it slides back down a foot. How many days will it take the spider to get to the top of the well?

Odd Word Out

Which of the following words is different from the others, and why?

THEFT, WAIL, GROSS, LAKE, MILE

Stretching the String

You tie a five-pound weight to a string and tie the string to the ceiling. The string successfully holds the five-pound weight in place. You untie the five-pound weight and attach a six-pound weight. The string snaps immediately under the weight.

If you were to use the same string, tie a four-pound weight to each end, and put the two ends on either side of a pulley, would the string hold or break?

The Hilbert Hotel

The German mathematician David Hilbert dreamed up the idea of a Grand Hotel with an infinite number of rooms and an infinite number of guests staying in the rooms.

Suppose a person enters the lobby of the Grand Hotel and asks the receptionist if there are any free rooms. "I'm afraid every room has a guest in it," the receptionist replies, "but I can still guarantee you a room to yourself." Once this guest is taken care of, a tour bus pulls up outside the Grand Hotel carrying an infinite number of passengers. The driver of the bus approaches the receptionist and asks if there are any free rooms for the infinite number of guests on the bus. "I'm afraid every room has a guest in it," the receptionist replies again, "but I can still guarantee each one of your passengers a room of his or her own."

How does the receptionist manage these feats?

Floating in Orbit

Why do astronauts on the International Space Station orbiting the earth experience weightlessness?

Pascal's Triangle

The triangle drawn below was first invented by the philosopher and mathematician Blaise Pascal. Can you figure out the pattern according to which it was made and fill in the next row of digits?

```
            1
          1   1
        1   2   1
      1   3   3   1
    1   4   6   4   1
```

Connected Shapes

Which of the following shapes is different from the four others, and how?

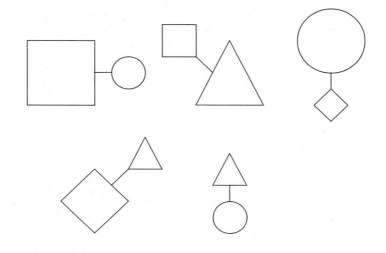

Enemies and Friends

"The enemy of my enemy is my friend."

If this statement is true, is it possible to be your own enemy?

A Question of Symmetry

Which of the following shapes is different from the four others, and how?

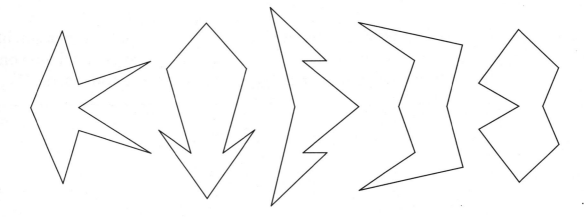

Life on Earth

What is wrong with the following argument? Do you know the name of the principle that exposes the fallacy in this kind of reasoning?

"The earth is just the right size and is situated just the right distance from a sun of just the right size in order to support life. That we should have come into being on a planet that is so ideally suited to supporting life cannot be just a coincidence."

Counting Rectangles

How many rectangles can you count in the figure below? Note that a square is a rectangle.

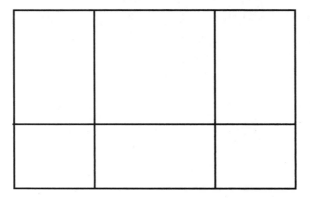

Finding Fossils

What is wrong with the following reasoning?

"Fossils of animals that lived about 100 million years ago are, on average, much larger than the animals living today. We can conclude that on the whole, animals were much larger 100 million years ago than they are today."

Purchasing an Automobile

"Every car with a manual transmission is made by Ford."
"I dislike cars that don't have a sporty design."
"No car with a sporty design has an automatic transmission."

Given the premises above, which of the following conclusions is true?

"I like only cars made by Ford."
"I like most cars made by Ford."
"I like no cars made by Ford."

The Tattooed Logicians

Two logicians are on holiday in the Alps when a mad scientist captures them. The mad scientist knocks them unconscious and then tattoos their foreheads. When they awake, the mad scientist says with a sneer:

"At least one of you has a tattoo on your forehead. Maybe both of you do—I'm not telling. I will allow you to go free if you have a tattoo on your forehead. All you have to do is walk out that door. However, if you walk out that door and you don't have a tattoo on your forehead, I will put you to death. I will leave you in this room and if you communicate with one another in any way, you will be put to death. Every day at noon, I will have the door unlocked briefly. You can choose to leave then and only then if you think you have a tattoo on your forehead."

How do the logicians escape and how long does it take them?

Picking Berries

Consider the following premises:

"The only berries I will discourage you from picking in this forest are the ones that are poisonous."
"All the red-colored berries are tasty."
"None of the berries on thorny bushes are poisonous."
"I discourage you from picking any berries that are not red."

If each of the above premises is true, which of the following conclusions is true?

"All of the red-colored berries are on thorny bushes."
"All of the berries on thorny bushes are tasty."
"None of the red-colored berries are poisonous."

Prisoner's Dilemma

Divide the class into pairs to play this game.

In each round, you and your partner will each write either *cooperate* or *compete* (whichever you want) on separate slips of paper. Make sure that your partner cannot see what you're writing. You will then show your slips of paper to each other at the same time. If you both cooperate, you both win three points. If you both compete, you both win one point. If one of you competes and the other cooperates, the one who chose to cooperate will win no points and the one who chose to compete will win five points.

You are not allowed to communicate with your partner in any way that will allow you to negotiate or agree on some sort of compromise. The game ends at a random moment indicated by the teacher. You never know which round will be the last.

After the game has ended, discuss it with your partner. Can you identify any strategies that could maximize your score?

DAILY SPARK   CRITICAL THINKING

Middle of the Class

On a certain math test, Jerry gets both the tenth-highest score in his class and the tenth-lowest score. If every student has a different score, how many students are there in the class?

Dots on Grids

The positioning of the two shaded squares on the three grids below follows a specific rule. Try to identify this rule and guess where the shaded squares should be on the fourth grid in this series.

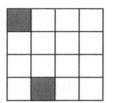 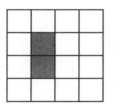 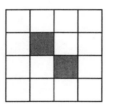 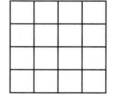

Kill 'Em All

What's wrong with the following argument?

"Theresa opposes the death penalty. That means she values the life of a killer more than she values the life of the person killed."

Purchasing Tickets

Consider the following premises:

"None of the tickets that have already been paid for are still on sale."
"No one can leave here with a ticket unless it has been stamped by an attendant."
"None of the tickets are stamped unless they have already been paid for."

If these three premises are true, which of the following conclusions is also true?

"Someone is forbidden to leave only if he or she has a ticket that is still on sale."
"No one can leave with a ticket that is still on sale."

All Squared Away

Which of the following numbers is different from the others, and how?

100, 300, 400, 900, 81, 25, 3600

The Illogic of Anti-Semitism

In October 2003, the outgoing Prime Minister of Malaysia, Mahathir Mohammed, addressed a summit of Islamic nations, declaring that Jews run the world. Many of those present applauded his speech, which he took as vindication of his views. Later, leaders, intellectuals, and activists around the world condemned Mahathir's speech as anti-Semitic. Mahathir responded by saying, "The reaction of the world shows that [Jews] control the world."

What is wrong with Mahathir's reasoning?

Shaping Up

Which of the following shapes is different from the others, and how? Do you know the name of the property that all the other shapes have in common?

   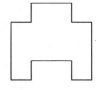

Hint: Imagine trying to use each of these shapes as a wallpaper pattern.

Separating the Circles

In the diagram below, draw three straight lines dividing the box into seven areas, each of which contains one circle.

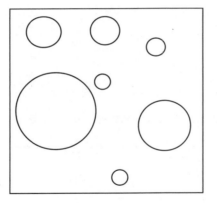

Funding Education

What is wrong with the following argument?

"Tuition fees are much higher than most students can afford. We must do something to help out the students. Therefore, we must support the new education bill."

Pieces of Square

Look at the three diagrams below. By drawing one line through a square, we can divide it into two parts. By drawing a second line through a square, we can divide it into a maximum of four parts. By drawing a third line through a square, we can divide it into a maximum of seven parts.

How many parts can we make by dividing a square with four lines? What about five lines? Do you see any pattern emerging?

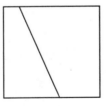 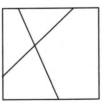 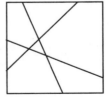

Becoming President

There are four prerequisites for becoming the President of the United States. First, you must be at least thirty-five years old. Second, you must have been born in the United States. Third, you must have been a resident of the United States for at least fourteen years.

What is the fourth prerequisite?

Hint: This fourth prerequisite is the most important of the four for preserving the democratic freedoms of the United States.

Let's Look at Towels

Why are bath towels shaggy instead of smooth?

DAILY SPARK   CRITICAL THINKING

© 2004 SparkNotes LLC

Racing Donkeys

A father dies, leaving this will:

"I have two daughters, each of whom owns a donkey. My daughters must race the donkeys from our town to the next, and the daughter whose donkey comes in second will receive everything I own."

The two daughters obediently get on their donkeys and head toward the next town. Both want to win the inheritance, of course, so both urge their donkeys to go as slowly as possible. After four hours, the two donkeys have barely advanced a hundred yards. The two daughters pause for lunch and are complaining about how long this "race" will take when a wise old woman crosses their path. When they tell her their story, the wise old woman gives them two words of advice. No sooner has she spoken than the daughters are racing the two donkeys toward the town as fast as they can.

What did the wise old woman say?

Mouse Catching

If it takes five cats five minutes to catch five mice, how many cats are needed to catch one hundred mice in one hundred minutes?

Scoring the Students

In both Appletown and Orangeville, 222 high school seniors take the SAT. The chart below shows how the students performed.

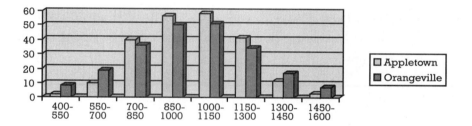

One of the members of the Orangeville Teachers Association boasts that Orangeville students are clearly brighter than Appletown students, given how many more Orangeville students scored above 1300 on their SATs.

Do you agree with this teacher's reasoning? Why or why not?

Colorful Clothing

Tanya has seven pairs of socks, seven pairs of pants, and seven shirts, one for each color of the rainbow. She wants to get a pair of socks, a pair of pants, and shirt out of her clothes drawer, and she wants to make sure they're all of different colors. If she doesn't open her eyes, how many items of clothing will she have to remove in order to be sure that she'll have one of each different color? A pair of socks counts as two items of clothing (in a pair of socks, each sock is the same color).

DAILY SPARK CRITICAL THINKING

© 2004 SparkNotes LLC

The Problem of the Gordian Knot

As Alexander the Great marched his armies across Asia Minor, he heard a story about the town of Gordium, where an ingenious knot secured an oxcart to a post. According to legend, the person who could detach the cart from the post would unite Europe and Asia under a single empire. To date, not even the most brilliant minds had managed to find a way of untying the Gordian Knot.

Alexander made his way to Gordium. He was no great knot specialist, but when he arrived he quickly separated the two ropes, much to the astonishment of the townsfolk, and went on to establish the largest empire the world had yet seen.

How did Alexander solve the problem of the Gordian Knot?

A Young Mother

Dora recently celebrated her eighth birthday, and yet she already has three children. She gave birth to all three, and she has celebrated her birthday every year that it came around. How is this possible?

Sorting Out the Relatives

What relationship do the following people have to you?

1) Your only uncle's only brother's only child
2) Your mother's sister's daughter's only cousin
3) Your maternal grandmother's son's only brother-in-law's child

Jam Today

Consider the following passage from *Through the Looking-Glass*, by Lewis Carroll:

"I'm sure I'll take *you* with pleasure!" the Queen said. "Two pence a week and jam every other day."

Alice couldn't help laughing, as she said, "I don't want you to hire *me*—and I don't care for jam."

"It's very good jam," said the Queen.

"Well, I don't want any *today*, at any rate."

"You couldn't have it if you *did* want it," the Queen said. "The rule is, jam tomorrow and jam yesterday—but never jam *today*."

"It *must* come sometimes to 'jam today,'" Alice objected.

"No, it can't," said the Queen. "It's jam every *other* day: today isn't any other day, you know."

What is fishy about the Queen's reasoning?

Smelly Dogs

Consider the following three premises:

"All unwashed dogs are smelly."
"All these terriers smell good."
"No dog running free in the park has been washed."

If all these premises are true, which of the following conclusions is necessarily true?

"No terrier is running free in the park."
"All the dogs that have been washed are terriers."
"All the dogs that aren't terriers are running free in the park."

Connect the Vertices

There are no lines you can draw connecting the vertices of a triangle that cut across the triangle. There are two lines you can draw connecting the vertices of a square that cut across the square. There are five lines you can draw connecting the vertices of a pentagon that cut across the pentagon. These facts are illustrated below:

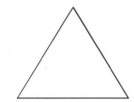 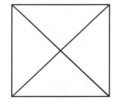 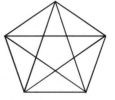

How many lines could you draw connecting the vertices of a hexagon? What about a seven-sided figure? Do you see any pattern emerging? Without drawing one, can you calculate how many lines could be drawn connecting the vertices of an octagon?

DAILY SPARK   CRITICAL THINKING

Clock Watchers

How many times in a day will the minute hand and the hour hand of a clock point in exactly the same direction?

Thinking About Drinking

Alcoholic drinks are labeled to let consumers know how much alcohol is in the drink. Usually this is given as a percentage of the total volume of the drink.

If the alcohol content were listed in terms of a percentage of the total mass instead of the total volume, would this number be higher or lower? Note that a given volume of alcohol weighs more than the same volume of a nonalcoholic drink.

DAILY SPARK   CRITICAL THINKING

Mysterious Deaths

Mickey and Minnie are found dead on the floor, surrounded by water and broken glass. No weapons were used to kill them; they did not kill themselves.

How did Mickey and Minnie die?

Feeding on the Food Chain

In any ecosystem, there is a food chain in which certain organisms eat other organisms. For example, coyotes eat cats, cats eat spiders, spiders eat flies, and flies eat plants.

Which would have the greatest disruptive effect on an ecosystem containing coyotes, cats, spiders, flies, and plants: the disappearance of plants, the doubling of the number of plants, the disappearance of coyotes, or the doubling of the number of coyotes?

DAILY SPARK CRITICAL THINKING

© 2004 SparkNotes LLC

Registering Clefs

In a musical score, notes are arranged across five lines—called a staff—where notes on higher lines of the staff represent higher pitches. On the left-hand side of a staff, there is a clef symbol, which tells us which notes are represented by each line of the staff. Different instruments use different clef symbols because the most commonly played range of notes for any given instrument should always be in the middle of the staff.

Opposite are the three same notes represented in four different clefs: the bass, tenor, alto, and treble, respectively.

Musical scores for the violin, viola, cello, and double bass each use a different clef. The violin has the highest pitch of these four instruments, followed by the viola, cello, and double bass, in that order.

Based on this information, can you guess which instrument's scores are presented with which clef?

Answer the Question

Anil: You told me Franco was going to be at the party last night, but he just told me he never even planned to come.

Ted: Are you calling me a liar?

Anil: It's not quite that, I just want to understand—

Ted: Are you calling me a liar? Answer the question: yes or no?

What is unfair about Ted's questioning?

DAILY SPARK   CRITICAL THINKING

© 2004 SparkNotes LLC

Moving Perpetually

Albert invents what he thinks could be a world-changing machine. This machine heats a large container of water using a heating element underneath the container. When the water boils, the steam rises and pushes on a turbine that causes a metal rod to rotate. This rotating rod is used to generate electric energy. The steam meanwhile cools back into water and refills the container. What's ingenious about the machine is that some of the electric energy is routed to the heating element underneath the container of water. The energy created by the boiling water is then used to boil the water so that the machine can generate energy perpetually without any energy needing to be put into it.

But when Albert tries to patent his machine, he's met only with rejections. What's wrong with it?

Two Glasses

Randy has two drinking glasses with circular bases. The first glass is twice as tall as the second glass, and the second glass has a base with twice the radius of the first glass.

Which glass holds more water?

Crossing the River

A farmer has a fox, a chicken, and a bag of grain, and he needs to get all three across a river. He can only take one of these three across at a time. If he leaves the fox and the chicken alone on the same bank, the fox will eat the chicken. If he leaves the chicken and the grain alone on the same bank, the chicken will eat the grain. How can he get all three across?

Into the Woods

You're about to go on a weeklong hiking trip in the woods. Bearing in mind the rule of thumb that men should never carry more than one third of their body weight and women should never carry more than one quarter of their body weight, you decide to weigh your pack before you set off. But your backpack is big and lumpy, and you can't get it to stay on your bathroom scale without falling off. How can you find out how much your pack weighs?

DAILY SPARK   CRITICAL THINKING

Jumping Knights

In chess, each move a knight makes takes it two squares forward or back, and then one square right or left. For example, in one jump, a knight on square d4 in the diagram at right could jump to c2, b3, b5, c6, e6, f5, f3, or e2.

What's the fewest number of moves it would take to move a knight at d4 to each of the following squares?

d5, a3, b6, g4

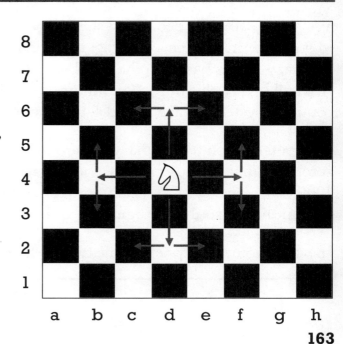

Counting Decimals

We count using the decimal system, meaning that there are ten different digits in our counting system. The fact that we use a decimal system is pretty much arbitrary, and is based on the number of fingers and thumbs we have on our hands. If we all had twelve fingers and thumbs, we would probably use a base-twelve counting system, which would actually make math a lot easier.

Computers often use a binary system, in which there are only two digits: one and zero. The first ten numbers in a binary system are: 1, 10, 11, 100, 101, 110, 111, 1000, 1001, and 1010. Basically, you're counting up all the numbers in the decimal system that use only the digits one and zero.

In which counting system is the twenty-fifth number 31?

Share the Love

If everybody loves anybody who loves somebody, under what circumstances would it *not* be true that everybody loves everybody?

Finding a Through-Line

If the line segment above the rectangle in the diagram below were traced across the rectangle, to which of the three line segments below the rectangle would it connect? Try to solve this problem without using a ruler.

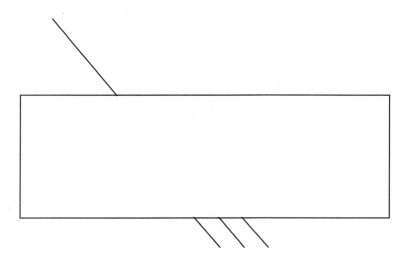

Counting the Triangles

How many triangles are there in the diagram below?

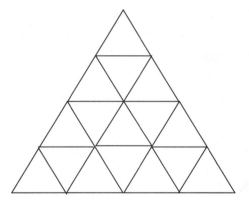

Shifting Gears

Below is a diagram of a simple set of bicycle gears. A metal chain would wrap around one of the two gears connected to the pedals and one of the two gears connected to the back wheel.

Which two gears would you want the chain to wrap around if you wanted to be able to pedal with the least effort?

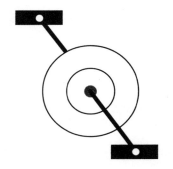 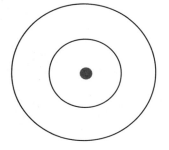

Match the Triangles

How can you arrange six matches in such a way that none of the matches cross over one another and that they also form four equilateral triangles?

Hint: Think of Egypt.

Russian Roulette

Jessica and Katie are forced by their captors to play a game of Russian roulette. Jessica gets a revolver with six chambers and puts two bullets into two adjacent chambers. She then spins the barrel, puts it against her head, and pulls the trigger. The gun doesn't fire. She passes the gun to Katie.

Katie can either put the gun against her head and pull the trigger, or she can spin the barrel first. Which gives her a better chance of survival?

Heavy Elephants

How would you weigh an elephant? Assume you don't have any scales that can bear the elephant's weight.

Frosty Killer

Agatha dashes into a police station and cries, "Help! Someone has murdered my friend Christie! I was walking by her house when suddenly I sensed that something terrible had happened. I went up to a first-floor window and wiped away the frost so I could look inside. Sure enough, Christie was lying dead on the floor!"

The police imediately arrest Agatha on suspicion of murder. Why?

Spare Change

What is the fewest number of coins you would need in order to make change for any amount of money between one cent and one dollar?

Sharing the Loot

Three thieves steal $1 million from a bank. When they get back to their secret hideout, the leader of the thieves says they're going to split up the money according to age-old bank robbery tradition. She reads a description of the tradition aloud:

"The leader of the thieves proposes a distribution plan for the loot. The band of thieves then votes on this proposal. If the majority of thieves vote against the proposal, then the leader is killed and the second-in-command becomes the new leader. The second-in-command must then make a new proposal, which all the thieves vote on, and if the majority votes against it, the second-in-command will also be killed, to be replaced by the third-in-command. This system continues until at least half of the thieves agree to a proposal, at which point the money is divided according to that proposal."

All the thieves are highly rational, and they all want to get as much money as they can without losing their lives. What distribution plan is the best proposal the leader can make?

Watching the Sunrise

Where on Earth does the sun not rise in the east?

Dark Forecast

A fortuneteller working the midnight shift tells one of her clients that in exactly one week, the sun will not shine. One week later, the client is amazed to find that the prediction was correct.

How did the fortuneteller do it?

DAILY SPARK CRITICAL THINKING

Fixing Squares

Below are two squares, one divided into four segments.

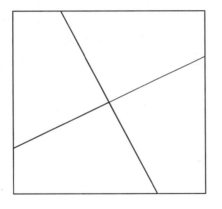

Rearrange the five pieces (four segments of one square plus the other square) so that they fit together to form a larger square. You may move the segments about however you please, but you cannot rotate or flip any of them.

What Do You Know?

What is wrong with the following claim?

"All knowledge can be divided into two classes. There is knowledge based on what we see, hear, smell, taste, and touch, and there is the abstract, deductive knowledge of logic and mathematics. Anything that falls outside these two classes cannot count as knowledge and is strictly meaningless."

DAILY SPARK   CRITICAL THINKING

Slamming Lockers

At Spark Central High School, the students have a bizarre last-day-of-school ritual. All one hundred students line up at their lockers, which are numbered one through a hundred. First, they all open their lockers. Second, the students at lockers two, four, six, eight, and so forth slam their lockers shut. Third, the people at every third locker starting at locker three toggle their lockers. That is, if their locker is shut, they open it, and if their locker is closed, they open it. Fourth, the people at every fourth locker starting at locker four toggle their lockers. This continues until the hundredth person toggles his locker.

When this ritual is complete, how many lockers will be open?

Trouble with the Pigpen

The pig in the diagram below has escaped from its pigpen. What can you do to put this paper pig back in its paper pigpen?

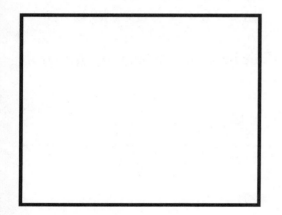

DAILY SPARK   CRITICAL THINKING

© 2004 SparkNotes LLC

Answers

1. The mistake is that "nothing" is being used in two different senses. In the first sentence, "nothing" is shorthand for "*having* nothing," but in the second sentence, "nothing" means simply "nothing." The mistake (or deliberate tactic) of using the same term to mean two different things over the course of an argument is called **equivocation**.

2. In the room with the light switches, switch on two of the lights. After ten minutes, switch one of the lights off and then go into the room with the light bulbs. One of the light bulbs will be on, and two will be off. The one that was recently turned off will still be hot, while the one that was never turned on will be cold.

3. Point to one of the two doors and ask either of the two guards, "According to the *other* guard, does this door lead to paradise?" The answer you get will always be untrue because the truthful guard will truthfully tell you the other guard's lie, while the lying guard will say the opposite of what the truthful guard would say. So if the guard says the door does not lead to paradise, you know it does; if the guard says the door does lead to paradise, you know it does not.

4. Caliph Omar committed the fallacy of a **false dilemma**. That is, he offered two possible alternatives and assumed they were the *only* alternatives. In fact, the books in the library might have neither contradicted nor agreed with the Koran. They might have dealt with subjects unrelated to the Koran.

5. You must be wearing a yellow hat. Juanita realizes that if both she and you were wearing yellow hats, Juan would have been able to deduce that he was wearing a blue hat, because there were only two yellow hats in the box. She can only be certain that she is wearing a blue hat because she sees that you are wearing a yellow hat and that Juan can't deduce the color of his own hat.

6. The answer is (b). If the length of the string is $2\pi r$, where r is the radius of the Earth, then the lengthened string has a length of $2\pi r + 1$m. In both cases, we can determine the distance of the string from the center of the Earth by dividing its length by 2π. With the original string, the distance is $2\pi r/2\pi = r$, which means the string is at the surface of the Earth, as we had assumed. With the lengthened string, the distance is $(2\pi r = 1\text{m})/2\pi = r + 1/2\pi$m. That is, the string is $1/2\pi \approx 0.159$m, or approximately 16 centimeters, above the surface of the Earth. Of course, none of these calculations are necessary as long as we recognize that the distance the string will rise from the surface of the Earth is roughly equal to the length we add to the string, and certainly not millions of times greater or less.

7. There is a fatal flaw in Bob's argument. Suppose Bob were to build a second computer, identical to this first one, and then make the two computers play against one another. One computer will beat the other, so clearly one of them will not have won every game it ever plays.

8. Move the horizontal toothpick to the left (the same solution is possible by moving it to the right) so that it lines up perpendicularly, touching end-to-end, with the bottom toothpick. Then move the top right toothpick so that it is parallel to the bottom toothpick and its end touches the other end of the horizontal toothpick. The result produces a new glass with the marble outside of it, as in the diagram at right.

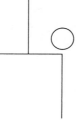

9. Each line refers to the previous line and describes the numbers in it. For example, the second-to-last line contains three ones, two twos, and then one one. The following line therefore reads "three ones, two twos, one one," or "312211." The next line in the sequence would describe this line, which contains one three, one one, two twos, and two ones, hence "13112221."

10. Whatever the smallest number that cannot be described in fewer than thirteen words is, there is a possible description of it that would only take up twelve words: "the smallest number that cannot be described in fewer than thirteen words."

11. Red objects seen through a red lens will be invisible, while blue objects seen through a red lens will appear purple. Similarly, blue objects seen through a blue lens will be invisible, while red objects seen through a blue lens will appear purple. As a result, your left eye will see blue lines as purple and your right eye will see red lines as purple, while the left eye will not be able to see red lines at all and the right eye will not be able to see blue lines at all. Because the blue lines and the red lines are slightly offset, your left eye will see the same purple image as the right eye, only slightly offset. Your eyes will naturally focus to make the purple images match up with one another, simulating the act of focusing on objects that are nearer or farther away. The more offset the blue and red images are, the closer they will appear in three-dimensional space when the eye tries to focus on them.

12. Nothing.

13. The solution is a matter of "thinking outside the box":

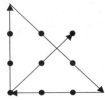

14. They fill the five-gallon jug and pour as much of it as possible into the three-gallon jug. That leaves two gallons left in the five-gallon jug. They empty the three-gallon jug and pour the two gallons remaining in the five-gallon jug into the three-gallon jug. Then they fill the five-gallon jug once more. Since there are now two gallons in the three-gallon jug, it will take only an additional gallon to fill the three-gallon jug. Once that is done, there will be four gallons left in the five-gallon jug.

15. Two wolves travel to the right bank. One wolf returns to the left bank. That wolf picks up the other wolf and goes to the right bank, so that all three wolves are on the right bank. One wolf returns to the left bank. Two lambs get in the boat and travel to the right bank. One lamb and one wolf get in the boat and travel to the left bank. Two lambs travel to the right bank, so that all three lambs and one wolf are now on the right bank. Now the wolf on the right bank can make two trips over to the left bank, picking up one wolf on each trip.

16. There will be nine berets in front of the first cadet, so there will be an odd number of one color and an even number of the other. If the first cadet says "red" it means she sees an even number of red berets in front of her, and if she says "blue" it means she sees an even number of blue berets in front of her. If, for instance, the second cadet hears "red" and sees an odd number of red berets in front of her, she will know she must be wearing one of the red berets and can call out "red" as well. The third cadet will have heard "red" twice, so she will know that the second cadet saw an odd number of red berets. If she too sees an odd number of red berets, she will know that she must be wearing a blue beret and can call out "blue." This system can perpetuate itself up the line so that all but the first cadet guesses correctly.

17. The mistake lies in dividing both sides by $x^2 - xy$. Since $x = y$, $x^2 - xy = 0$. Any number divided by 0 will be undefined, so the last step in the proof doesn't make sense.

18. The argument tries to prove that God exists by saying that the Bible is infallible because it is the word of God. But to argue that the Bible is the word of God assumes that God exists, which is the very point being argued. This sort of fallacy is called **begging the question.**

19. On the summer solstice, the sun is directly above the Tropic of Cancer, so a stick placed in the ground there would cast no shadow. As shown in the diagram below, the line drawn between the top of the stick Eratosthenes put in the ground and the top of its shadow on the ground will be parallel to a line drawn from the center of the earth to the Tropic of Cancer. That means that the angle between the stick and the line drawn from the top of the stick to the top of the shadow is equal to the angle between a line from the center of the earth to the Tropic of Cancer and a line from the center of the earth to the point where Eratosthenes puts his stick in the

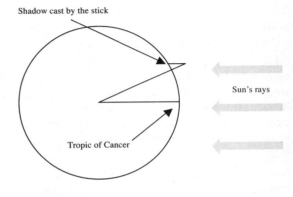

Shadow cast by the stick

Sun's rays

Tropic of Cancer

ground. Once he knew this angle, and the distance between his stick and the Tropic of Cancer, Eratosthenes could make a simple calculation to determine the full circumference of the earth.

20. No. If it were true, then Epimenides—himself a Cretan—would be a liar, and so the statement would be false. If it is false, then Epimenides himself may be a liar, but there are other Cretans who are not liars.

21. A pound of feathers and a pound of lead weigh the same amount: one pound. A pound of gold, however, weighs less than a pound of lead. Precious metals are weighed according to the

troy system of weights and measures, and one troy pound is slightly less than one standard—avoirdupois—pound.

22. You will be in second place. You have to pass the person in first place to be in first.

23. You would need four colors. There are only two sets of four countries on a world map that would each need to be a different color: Paraguay, Argentina, Bolivia, Brazil; and France, Belgium, Luxembourg, and Germany.

24. The easiest example of a surface where more than four colors could be needed is a *torus*, or donut. Imagine two rings of different colors that wrap around the donut, touching one another. That's two colors. Then imagine three strips that wrap around the rest of the donut length-wise so that they touch the two rings at both ends. These three strips are all touching one another and all touch both of the other two colors, so a fifth color is needed to distinguish the five areas from one another.

25. Seven. There is a one-in-six chance of rolling a seven, because there are several combinations that result in seven. You could roll a six on one die and a one on the other, a two on one die and a five on the other, or a three on one die and a four on the other. In contrast, there is only a one-in-thirty-six chance of rolling either a two or a twelve, because there is only one combination that results in a two (one and one) and one combination that results in a twelve (six and six).

26. The next number is 13. You get each number, besides the first two, by adding the previous two numbers in the sequence. This sequence, which has many mathematical applications, is called the **Fibonacci sequence**.

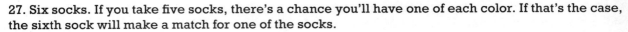

27. Six socks. If you take five socks, there's a chance you'll have one of each color. If that's the case, the sixth sock will make a match for one of the socks.

28. One possible set of counterexamples would be where A and B have a common cause, but are themselves unrelated. For example, at the beginning of the Second World War, Hitler invaded Poland. The English had given an ultimatum saying that if Hitler invaded Poland, England would declare war on Germany. Let A be "England declared war on Germany" and B be "The Germans captured Warsaw." Clearly, England declaring war on Germany was not the cause of Germany capturing Warsaw, but Germany would not have captured Warsaw without England declaring war because England had pledged to declare war if Germany invaded Poland.

29. There are three people: a grandfather, a father, and a son. Both the father and the grandfather are fathers, while the father is also the son of the grandfather.

30. Answers will vary. One possible set of answers is:
1. "All mammals are carnivores; lions are mammals; therefore, lions are carnivores."
2. "All lions are mammals; my dog is a lion; therefore, my dog is a mammal."
3. "All mammals are carnivores; alligators are mammals; therefore, alligators are carnivores."

31. Light one string at one end and the other string at both ends. The string that you've lit at both ends will be burned completely after half an hour, because two flames consume the string in half the time that one flame would. Once the string is completely burned, light the other end of the other string. After half an hour, that string would still take half an hour to burn with one flame, so it would take fifteen minutes to burn with two. Those fifteen minutes plus the half hour already elapsed come to forty-five minutes.

32. The two countries are Liechtenstein, which borders Switzerland and Austria, and Uzbekistan, which borders Kazakhstan, Kyrgyzstan, Tajikistan, Afghanistan, and Turkmenistan.

33. Most people with full-time jobs will be at work between 11 a.m. and 3 p.m. on a Monday, so a disproportionate number of people who were actually reached by phone were not full-time workers.

34. The South Pole. Traveling due south will lead back to the South Pole even if Roald had gone thirty miles west in the meantime. There are actually an infinite number of places on earth Roald could have placed his flag, the South Pole being only the most obvious. For example, Roald could have started a little less than thirty-five miles from the North Pole, planted the flag, walked thirty miles toward the North Pole and found himself at a place where walking a full circle around the North Pole would cover thirty miles. Walking that circle in a clockwise direction will make a thirty-mile trip in the westward direction and walking thirty miles south after walking that circle will get him back to the flag.

35. Helga is in the Pacific Ocean. While heading west, she crossed the International Date Line. She has been traveling for twenty-three hours and five minutes, but the time change is only five minutes.

36. Fifty percent, just like every other time. Previous flips of the coin have no influence on how the next flip will turn out.

37. The fewest number of moves is ten: from 382546197 to 528346197 to 438256197 to 283456197 to 823456197 to 165432897 to 234561897 to 654321897 to 981234567 to 765432189 to 123456789. A good general strategy is to try to flip the numbers in such a way that the leftmost number ends up next to the number one greater than it.

38. Answers will vary. Some possibilities include: pointing out that there would be no horizon if the earth were flat; showing photographs taken of the earth from space; or pointing out that the shadow cast by the earth on the moon during a lunar eclipse is round.

39. 91. The only non-prime, two-digit numbers that are not multiples of 2, 3, or 5 are 77 and 91. The two digits of 77 are the same, so it can only be 91.

40. Two. First, put three marbles in one pan and three marbles in the other. If the two pans balance each other out, you know that the heavier marble is among the three you didn't measure. Otherwise, it's among the three that outweigh the other three. Once you have narrowed it down to three marbles, you put one marble in each of the pans. If one of the two marbles is heavier, you've found the heavier marble, and if the two marbles weigh the same, you know the heavier marble must be the one you didn't weigh.

41. Men in their seventies are more likely to die than men in their twenties because they are far more susceptible to cancer, heart attacks, and other leading causes of death. The fact that suicide falls behind these other causes of death as men get older does not in itself indicate that fewer older men commit suicide. In fact, men in their seventies have a suicide rate nearly twice that of men in their twenties.

42. Alba and Bobo run across: two minutes. Alba runs back: one minute. Coco and Dodo run across: ten minutes. Bobo runs back: two minutes. Alba and Bobo run across: two minutes. Total: seventeen minutes.

43. As shown in the diagram at right, the sun's rays strike the earth dead on at the equator, while they strike the earth at a greater angle the closer they are to the poles. As a result, the energy absorbed from the sun closer to the poles is only a fraction of the energy absorbed at the equator.

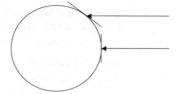

44. You would have written more 2s, because every number between 200,000 and 299,999 begins with a 2, while the numbers in the hundred thousands beginning with 7 are all greater than 500,000.

45. If you know exactly when the sun rises and sets at a particular place—Greenwich, England, in Harrison's case—and carry with you a chronometer set to the time in that place, you can measure the time difference between your present location and the location at which your chronometer was set. If you are at the same latitude as your original location and the sun sets an hour later than it would at your original location, you know that you are one twenty-fourth of the earth's circumference, or fifteen degrees of longitude, west of your original location.

46. Yes. Seven family members multiplied by three bowls of rice equals a total of twenty-one bowls of rice. He can feed his family sixteen bowls of rice, and scrape another four bowls from the leftovers. From those four bowls, he can scrape another bowl's worth of leftovers, making a total of 16 + 4 + 1, or twenty-one bowls of rice.

47. Answers will vary.

48. The doctor is the boy's mother.

49. If you are going second, always do the opposite of what your partner does. If your partner circles two dots, you circle one, and if your partner circles one dot, you circle two. That way, each round you'll circle three dots between the two of you. After three rounds, you'll have circled nine dots, leaving your partner with the final dot.

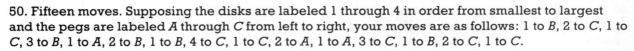

50. Fifteen moves. Supposing the disks are labeled 1 through 4 in order from smallest to largest and the pegs are labeled *A* through *C* from left to right, your moves are as follows: 1 to *B*, 2 to *C*, 1 to *C*, 3 to *B*, 1 to *A*, 2 to *B*, 1 to *B*, 4 to *C*, 1 to *C*, 2 to *A*, 1 to *A*, 3 to *C*, 1 to *B*, 2 to *C*, 1 to *C*.

51. The analogy between government and business breaks down because a business, unlike government, exists primarily to benefit the people running and working for it. We would like to think that a government exists primarily to benefit the people it serves, not the people running it.

52. Answers may vary. One possible set of answers: if you run a magnet over the contents of the bowl, it will pick up the iron filings and separate them from the other two ingredients. Then you might pour water into the bowl and stir it all up. The sugar will dissolve in the water, leaving only the mustard seeds at the bottom. Once you have separated the sugar-water and the mustard seeds, you can boil the water so that all the water evaporates and only the sugar remains.

53. Water freezes at 32°F. Salt water freezes at 15°F. If the salt is sprinkled on an icy patch of road or sidewalk, the ice will absorb the salt and may melt. That makes roads and sidewalks less slippery.

54. This argument contains the mistake of **equivocation**—taking one word to mean two different things. The Declaration of Independence uses the word equal to mean "equal before the law," whereas this argument uses the word *equal* to mean "equal in all innate attributes."

55. The fact that so many presidents elected in years ending with a zero have died in office is purely coincidental. That is, none of these presidential deaths is in any way linked to the year of the president's election. The argument can only carry weight if some causal link is identified between the year of election and the fate of the president.

56. No. He hasn't done anything about the eleventh brother.

Answers *DAILY SPARK   CRITICAL THINKING*

191

57. "I am going to have my head chopped off." If that statement is false, you will be condemned to having your head chopped off, making the statement true. If it is true, you will be condemned to the electric chair, making the statement false. So neither form of execution is applicable in your case.

58. Global warming is expected to result in a gradual increase in temperature, showing an overall rise in temperature over many years. Since it is only a general trend, one year of colder temperatures in itself is no proof against it, just as one year of warmer temperatures would be no proof in its favor.

59. The problem was worded deceptively. The three sisters have paid a total of $27 to the restaurant. The waiter has kept $2 and the restaurant has kept $25. So we shouldn't be adding the waiter's $2 to the sisters' $27 to determine how much money there is, but rather adding the waiter's $2 to the amount the restaurant charged ($25) to see what it adds up to. It should add up to $30 minus the $3 the waiter returned to the sisters—$27, that is—which it does.

60. No. Moscow has a population more than ten times that of Washington, D.C. As a result, the actual murder rate in Moscow is less than half the murder rate in Washington, D.C.

61. Answers may vary. One easy approach would be to get some sort of surface, like a board, preferably dark in color so that the snowflakes would stand out more easily. It would be best to chill this surface in a freezer so that snowflakes didn't melt upon making contact with it. Sally could leave this surface outside for a specified period of time—say, a minute—and count how many snowflakes fell on this surface over the course of a minute. She could then multiply that number of snowflakes by the number of minutes in the day, and by the total size of the farm divided by the size of the surface. The resulting number would likely be greater than 1 billion.

62. None. All the birds that survived have flown away.

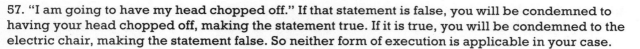

63. Store A's performance only looks twice as strong as B's because of the small increments shown on the graph. In fact, Store A sold 196 units while Store B sold 188 units, so the difference is almost negligible.

64. In every set of five apples that Ed is selling for two dollars, he's selling three of the apples priced at three for a dollar and two of the apples priced at two for a dollar. Consequently, after selling fifty apples at five for two dollars, Ed has sold twenty of the apples priced at two for a dollar and all thirty of the apples priced at three for a dollar. What remains are ten apples, all of which should be sold at two for a dollar. By selling those remaining ten at five for two dollars, he's making less money than he should.

65. Lions. The first islander must have said he had eagles on his feet: if he did have eagles on his feet he would have told the truth, and if he had lions on his feet he would have lied and said he had eagles. That means the second islander was telling the truth when she translated him as saying he had eagles on his feet. Because she's truthful, she must have eagles on her feet. Since she has eagles on her feet, the third islander was lying when he said she had lions, so, as a liar, he must have lions on his feet.

66. There is no single solution, but all of the solutions require that you start at one of the bottom corners and end at the other bottom corner.

67. A hole.

68. Put one blue marble in one of the boxes and all the rest of the marbles in the other box. There's a fifty-fifty chance that the executioner will choose the box with the blue marble, in which case your life will be spared. And if the executioner chooses the other box, there's still nearly a fifty-fifty chance (49 in 99, to be precise) that your life will still be spared. In all, you have a nearly three in four chance of survival.

69. The first sequence is a series of square numbers, so 8 should be replaced by 9. The second sequence adds one sixth each time, so 4/5 should be replaced by 5/6. The third sequence is a sequence of prime numbers, so 10 should be replaced by 11.

70. Paolo's house is at the South Pole. Every direction is north at the South Pole.

71. Answers will vary. A number of philosophers since Wittgenstein have attempted to give definitions that have no counterexamples, but none of these definitions is universally accepted.

72. Seven: four boys and three girls. Each boy has three brothers and three sisters, and each girl has four brothers and two sisters.

73. First of all, it is possible that there is an as yet undiscovered valid proof of God's existence. It is also possible that there is no proof of God's existence but that God exists nonetheless. The argument in the prompt establishes that we cannot be certain that God exists, but it does not establish that we can be certain that God does *not* exist.

74. Counterfeit money.

75. The speaker is making an *ad hominem* attack on Jack. That is, he's attacking Jack's character rather than his arguments. The fact that Jack is a coward has no bearing on whether or not his arguments are valid.

76. He doesn't need to outrun the tiger in order to survive. He only needs to outrun the other explorer.

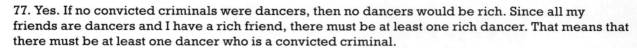

77. Yes. If no convicted criminals were dancers, then no dancers would be rich. Since all my friends are dancers and I have a rich friend, there must be at least one rich dancer. That means that there must be at least one dancer who is a convicted criminal.

78. The water level falls. While the ball bearing was in the box, and hence floating on the water, it displaced an amount of water equal to its mass. When it sits at the bottom of the water, it displaces only an amount of water equal to its volume. Since ball bearings are denser than water, a volume of water equal to the volume of the ball bearing will not have as much mass as an amount of water equal to the mass of the ball bearing.

79. The competitor reasons that if he were wearing a pink hat, each of the other two competitors would see one person wearing a green hat and one person wearing a pink hat. They could then reason that they must be wearing a green hat, because if they were wearing a pink hat, the person in the green hat would not see any green hats and so would not have raised her hand. Because no one raised his or her hand for a couple of minutes, the competitor reasons that he can't be wearing a pink hat, or else one of the others would have won. Therefore, he must be wearing a green hat.

80. Two inches. Remember, when three books are placed on a shelf, the first page of the first book will be the one closest to the second book, as will be the last page of the last book. So the distance between the two pages is the width of one book (one inch) + the width of four bindings (¼ inch x 4 = 1 inch).

81. Arrange the buttons so that there is one button on top of the other in the top right corner, as shown below.

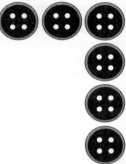

82. X. The sequence is the sequence of Roman numerals.

83. Put one coin from the first bag, two coins from the second bag, three coins from the third bag, four coins from the fourth bag, and five coins from the fifth bag on the weighing scale at once. That makes a total of fifteen coins, so if all the coins weigh ten grams, the total will come to 150 grams. If the total comes to 149 grams, you know that just one of the coins is lighter than the others, so you know the lighter coins are in the first bag. If the total comes to 148 grams, you can reason similarly that the lighter coins are in the second bag. If the total comes to 147 grams, the lighter coins are in the third bag, if the total comes to 146 grams, the lighter coins are in the fourth bag, and if the total comes to 145 grams, the lighter coins are in the fifth bag.

84. Light travels faster than sound; sound travels faster than bullets; so (b), then (c), then (a).

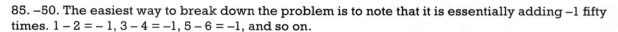

85. −50. The easiest way to break down the problem is to note that it is essentially adding −1 fifty times. $1 - 2 = -1, 3 - 4 = -1, 5 - 6 = -1$, and so on.

86. Answers will vary. One set of possible answers is given here.
Photograph: photos can't lie, but the photographer has expressed an opinion merely by choosing the angle and the shot, which means the photo isn't totally objective.
Eyewitness account: the person was there and can give a personal account, but the person may not be objective or remember everything accurately.
Textbook: While textbooks draw on a number of different sources, they can reflect the editor's biases.
News broadcast: news reporters tend to be less biased in their accounts than actual participants, but they may leave out messy details in an effort to be easily accessible to a mainstream audience.

87. 4 p.m. If the area doubles every hour, the slide will be half-covered with bacteria an hour before it is completely covered.

88. The first premise says that all criminals carry guns. It doesn't say that *only* criminals carry guns, however. It's possible that Jerry isn't a criminal but still carries a gun.

89. No. The coin is clearly a counterfeit. In 47 B.C., the terminology "B.C." did not yet exist. B.C. stands for "Before Christ," so the people living in 47 B.C. could not have known that Christ would be born in forty-seven years.

90. This argument uses **equivocation**, which involves using a single term to mean two different things. In the first sentence, "no horse" is equivalent to "zero horses," while in the second sentence "no horse" is equivalent to "there is no horse that . . . ."

91. *E*. The letters in the sequence are the first letters of each number, counting up from one.

92. All the animals listed above can be found in the Arctic except for penguins. Penguins are only found in the southern hemisphere.

93. Tony said he wouldn't go out if there were a hockey game, but he didn't say that he would definitely join if there weren't a hockey game. The occurrence of a hockey game is perhaps only one of a number of conditions that would keep Tony from going out.

94. 6. Each number corresponds to the number of other regions bordering that region.

95. The color scheme repeats itself every fourth shape, while the shape scheme repeats itself every third shape, so the correct shape is this one:

96. One. The speaker is going to St. Ives. If he meets the man with his wives on the way, then the man and his wives are going in the opposite direction—away from St. Ives, that is.

97. They are standing in the following order, from left to right: Beatrice, Ernie, Andy, Colin, Florence, Danielle.

98. All the items in the list belong to the plant kingdom except for the mushroom, which is a fungus.

99. First, they must borrow a cow from their neighbor, because there is no way for the third son to receive one ninth of the cows without either having a number of cows divisible by nine or cutting up a cow. With the borrowed cow, the total number of cows comes to eighteen. One half of the eighteen cows, or nine cows, go to the oldest son, six cows go to the second son, and two cows go

to the third son, for a total of seventeen cows between the three of them. Then they return the cow they borrowed.

100. Zero. Any number multiplied by zero is zero.

101. The solution is 4 1 3 1 2 4 3 2, or the reverse.

102. The vertical line is only three-quarters the length of the horizontal line. The arrowheads pointing out from it create an optical illusion that makes it look longer.

103. The argument relies on setting up a **straw man** portrayal of the opposing position. If the only reason adults opposed underage drinking were that young people shouldn't have too much fun, the argument might hold water. But there are other, far better reasons for opposing underage drinking, and this argument fails to account for them.

104. No. Suppose A loves himself. In other words, A loves A. According to the premise, A cannot love anyone who is loved by A. So if A loves A, then A cannot love A. We find ourselves in a contradiction.

105. No. To stay in flight, the birds must push air down that is equal to their weight. The weight in the back of the truck remains constant.

106. This question presents a paradox. If this catalogue "of all the catalogues that do not list themselves" is listed within its own pages, then it is a catalogue that lists itself and therefore doesn't belong within its own pages. If this catalogue is not listed within its own pages, then it is a catalogue that does not list itself, so it does belong within its own pages.

107. Take a fruit out of the box labeled "apples and oranges." Since you know each box is mislabeled, you know that this box contains either only apples or only oranges. Removing one fruit from the box will determine which it contains. Place the label for the fruit you removed on that box. You can then confidently place the "apples and oranges" label on the box labeled with the name of the fruit that you didn't remove from the box, because you know that every box is mislabeled. Finally, by process of elimination, you can place the label for the fruit you didn't draw from the original "apples and oranges" box on the remaining box.

108. The solution is diagrammed here:

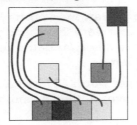

109. The pebble will be kicked directly upward. The car tire exerts a centripetal force on the pebble, accelerating it toward the center of the tire. Pebbles look like they are being kicked back from the car only because the car is moving forward while the pebbles are moving up and down in place.

110. Every iteration multiplies the perimeter by 4/3, so an infinite number of iterations will give the figure an infinite perimeter, even though its area will be finite.

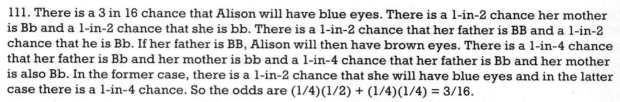

111. There is a 3 in 16 chance that Alison will have blue eyes. There is a 1-in-2 chance her mother is Bb and a 1-in-2 chance that she is bb. There is a 1-in-2 chance that her father is BB and a 1-in-2 chance that he is Bb. If her father is BB, Alison will then have brown eyes. There is a 1-in-4 chance that her father is Bb and her mother is bb and a 1-in-4 chance that her father is Bb and her mother is also Bb. In the former case, there is a 1-in-2 chance that she will have blue eyes and in the latter case there is a 1-in-4 chance. So the odds are (1/4)(1/2) + (1/4)(1/4) = 3/16.

112. Mrs. Egan can say, "Take that duck back into the kitchen and throw it out. And while you're in there, take the other duck out of the oven. It should be ready by now." Mr. Egan can then take the duck off the floor, return it to the kitchen, clean it off, and bring it back out as the "other duck."

113. You can: someone whom you admire will *not* admire you. Let's suppose it is possible that someone you admire, Ambika, also admires you. Since you admire everyone Ambika admires, that means you must also admire yourself. But, according to the second premise, you can't admire yourself. So the two premises lead to a contradiction; it is impossible that that someone whom you admire will also admire you.

114. Euthyphro has made a **circular**, or **tautological**, argument. He has said that things are holy because the gods approve of them, and that the gods approve of things because they are holy.

115. Nine. The net gain after each day and night is one foot (climbs two feet, loses one), so that after eight days, the spider will be eight feet up. On the ninth day, the spider will climb the last two feet to the rim of the well before nightfall.

116. All of the words except GROSS are composed only of letters without any curves. All of the letters in the word GROSS have curves in them.

117. The string would hold. The tension on the string at both ends is the same as if each four-pound weight were suspended from the ceiling independently. Given that the string can support a five-pound weight, it can certainly support a four-pound weight.

118. When the first guest arrives, the receptionist asks each one of the guests already occupying a room to move to the next one up. That is, the person in room 1 moves to room 2, the person in room 2 moves to room 3, and so on. Then the receptionist puts the new guest in room 1. When the infinite tour bus arrives, the receptionist asks the guests already in the hotel to move to the hotel room whose number is twice the number of their present room. That is, the person in room 1 moves to room 2, the person in room 2 moves to room 4, and so on. Then the receptionist puts all the guests from the infinite tour bus into all the rooms with odd numbers. The receptionist is taking advantage of the fact that there are as many natural numbers as there are even numbers. These are just some of the strange quirks of infinity.

119. Because the space station is in perpetual freefall. Objects remain in orbit because they are falling very fast and at an angle to the earth such that they are pulled around the earth rather than down to its surface. It's a common misconception that satellites in orbit, and astronauts on board them, are weightless because they are too far from the earth's surface to experience the effects of gravity.

120. The outer two digits in any row are 1s. All the other digits are the sum of the two digits above them. Thus, the next row would be 1 5 10 10 5 1.

121. All the shapes consist of a large shape connected to a small shape except for the last one, in which both the triangle and the circle are small.

122. No. If you are friends with all your enemy's enemies, you must be your own friend.

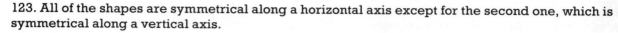

123. All of the shapes are symmetrical along a horizontal axis except for the second one, which is symmetrical along a vertical axis.

124. Even if it were a coincidence that Earth is ideally suited to supporting life, so much so that there is no other life-supporting planet in the universe, we as living beings would necessarily have to exist on Earth in order to wonder whether it's a coincidence. So our existence on a life-supporting planet cannot be taken as evidence of anything, since our existence on a non–life supporting planet is impossible. The principle that we should avoid biases in our observations that fail to factor out our own role as observers is called the **anthropic principle**.

125. Twenty. The large rectangle is divided up into six smaller cells. There are six rectangles comprising one cell, seven rectangles comprising two cells, two rectangles comprising three cells, two rectangles comprising four cells, and one rectangle comprising all eight cells.

126. We are far more likely to dig up fossils of larger animals because they are easier to find and more likely to be preserved. There may have been many smaller animals living 100 million years ago of which we have no fossil evidence.

127. "I like only cars made by Ford" is true. We can rephrase the second premise as "If I like a car, then it has a sporty design." We can rephrase the third premise as "If a car has a sporty design, then it has a manual transmission," since any car that doesn't have an automatic transmission will have a manual transmission. From these two rephrased premises, we can draw the conclusion, "If I like a car, then it has a manual transmission." Since, according to the first premise, every car with a manual transmission is made by Ford, we can conclude that if I like a car, it must be made by Ford.

128. It takes them two days. Each can see the tattoo on the other's forehead, so neither can be certain there's a tattoo on her own forehead. Consequently, neither tries to make an escape on the first day when the door is unlocked at noon. However, each reasons independently that if there were no tattoo on her own forehead, the other would have known for certain that there was a tattoo on her forehead and would have left that day. Since neither of them left on the first day, each is now certain that they have a tattoo on their own forehead, and so both of them leave the following day.

129. "All of the berries on thorny bushes are tasty" is true. We can rephrase the first premise as "If a berry is not poisonous I will not discourage you from picking it." We can rephrase the fourth premise as "If I do not discourage you from picking a berry, then it is red." Combining these two premises, we can conclude, "If a berry is not poisonous, then it is red." Since, according to the second premise, all red-colored berries are tasty, we can conclude, "If a berry is not poisonous, then it is tasty." And since, according to the third premise, none of the berries on thorny bushes are poisonous, we can infer that they are all tasty.

130. This game is one of the more basic elements of the very complex world of **game theory**. Unless one player knows how to take advantage of his partner consistently, the best strategy over the long term is cooperation. Mathematically, the best strategy to encourage your partner to maximize both scores is called "tit for tat." The principle is that you will always start by choosing the word "cooperate," but you will choose to the word "compete" in any round following a round in which your partner chose to the word "compete."

131. Nineteen. If there were twenty, then finishing tenth would give Jerry the eleventh lowest score.

Answers *DAILY SPARK   CRITICAL THINKING*

132. The shaded square that starts in the top left is moving progressively down and to the right, while the square that starts at the bottom of the second column is moving progressively up. The fourth grid should look like this one:

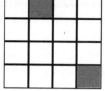

133. The argument relies implicitly on the assumption that Theresa thinks that the killer's life ought to be spared and that the person killed ought to have died. Theresa can coherently maintain her position simply by saying that she doesn't think that killing is right, even in revenge.

134. Rephrase the second premise as, "If you can leave, then your ticket has been stamped by an attendant." Rephrase the third premise as, "If your ticket has been stamped by an attendant, then it has been paid for." Combined the last two premises imply, "If you can leave, then your ticket has been paid for." The first premise can be rephrased, "If your ticket has been paid for, then it is not on sale," leading to the rephrased second conclusion: "If you can leave, then you do not have a ticket that is on sale." Note that the first of the possible conclusions is not identical to this claim, but is rather the inverse: "If you cannot leave, then you have a ticket that is still on sale."

135. All of the numbers except 300 are perfect squares.

136. Mahathir renders his reasoning **nonfalsifiable**. If people approve of his claim that Jews run the world, he takes it as evidence that he must be correct. If people disapprove of his claim that Jews run the world, he also takes it as evidence that he must be correct. As such, there is no evidence that could persuade Mahathir that he is mistaken. Hence, evidence ceases to have any value and his claim itself becomes meaningless.

137. All of the shapes except for the pentagon (the third shape) can be used to make **tessellations**, where multiple copies of the shape can be laid out in a pattern in which they all interlock and there are no gaps.

138. The solution is diagrammed below.

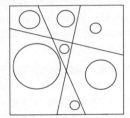

139. The conclusion that we must support the new education bill does not necessarily follow from the arguments that tuition is too high and that we must help the students. We might agree that students need to be helped without agreeing with the program outlined in the new education bill. The speaker has falsely equated support for the new education bill with a desire to help students.

140. You can divide a square into 11 parts with four lines and 16 parts with five lines. For the *n*th line that you draw, you will create *n* new areas. The formula for the maximum number of areas in a square with *n* lines is $n(n+1)/2 + 1$.

141. In order to become president, a person must have been elected to the office.

142. Cloth absorbs more water the greater its surface area is. Each piece of shag on a towel increases the towel's total surface area and hence its ability to absorb water.

143. "Trade donkeys."

144. Five. The five cats catch mice at a rate of one per minute, so five cats will be enough to catch one hundred mice in one hundred minutes.

145. The teacher's reasoning is flawed. There may be more Orangeville students who got top scores, but there are also more Orangeville students who got low scores. The Appletown students are more closely grouped around the average score of 1000, while the Orangeville students' scores are more widely distributed. On average, Appletown students actually scored slightly higher than Orangeville students.

146. Seven. If she takes out one pair of socks (two items of clothing) she will need to take out at least two pairs of pants in case one pair is the same color as the socks. Then she will need to take out three shirts in case the first two shirts are the same color as the pants.

147. He took out his sword and cut the knot in two. The challenge is simply to separate the two ropes. There is nothing in the story about having to untie the knot.

148. Dora was born on February 29. Consequently, her birthday comes around only once every four years. Though she has only celebrated eight birthdays, she has been alive for thirty-two years.

149. In all three cases, the person described is you yourself. Note that the word "only" makes all the difference. In the first instance, for example, you can't cite your cousin as a valid answer, because under the parameters of the question, you have only one uncle, who has only one brother (your father), and your father has only one child (you).

150. What we refer to when we say "tomorrow" today is the same day that we refer to when we say "today" tomorrow. By insisting that tomorrow we will have jam "tomorrow" and not "today," the Queen ignores the fact that the referents of words like "today" and "tomorrow"—as with the referents of "I," "here," or "now"—depend on the context of the utterance. For example, the words "today" and "tomorrow" refer to different days depending on the day on which they're spoken.

151. Rephrase the third premise as, "If a dog is running free in the park, then it has not been washed." Rephrase the first premise as, "If a dog has not been washed, then it is smelly." Rephrase the second premise as, "If a dog is smelly, then it is not a terrier." These three rephrased premises combine to form the third conclusion, which can be rephrased, "If a dog is running free in the park, then it is not a terrier." The fact that all the terriers are washed doesn't mean that all the washed dogs are terriers, so the second conclusion is not true. There may be dogs that aren't terriers that are nevertheless clean, so the first conclusion is not true.

152. You can draw nine lines across a hexagon, fourteen across a seven-sided figure, and twenty across an octagon. In calculating how many lines will cross an n-sided figure, you add a number one greater than the number you added for an $(n-1)$-sided figure. There are two more lines crossing a square than a triangle, three more lines crossing a pentagon than a square, four more lines crossing a hexagon than a pentagon, and so on. Mathematically speaking, we could say that, for a figure of n sides, there will be $n(n-3)/2$ lines crossing it.

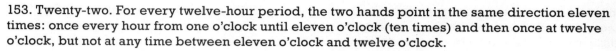

153. Twenty-two. For every twelve-hour period, the two hands point in the same direction eleven times: once every hour from one o'clock until eleven o'clock (ten times) and then once at twelve o'clock, but not at any time between eleven o'clock and twelve o'clock.

154. The percentage of total mass would give a higher number than the percentage of total volume. Suppose, for example, we were dealing with a drink that had 50% alcohol per volume. The half that was alcohol would weigh more than the half that wasn't alcohol, so more than half of the total mass would be alcohol.

155. Mickey and Minnie are fish; someone broke their tank.

156. The disappearance of plants. That would leave the flies with nothing to feed on, and if they died out, the spiders would have nothing to feed on, and so on up the food chain. The entire ecosystem would break down. The ecosystem would change somewhat with the other three possibilities, but it would ultimately find a new equilibrium.

157. The violin uses the treble clef, the viola uses the alto, the cello uses the tenor, and the double bass uses the bass clef. The treble clef is best suited for higher notes, as we can see, because the same notes in the treble clef are presented as much lower on the staff than in any of the other clefs.

158. Ted is distorting Anil's position in three ways. First, he's creating a false dilemma: either Anil is a liar or he isn't. In fact, there are other possibilities. For example, Anil may have told a lie on this one occasion even though he's generally honest. Second, Ted is changing the subject. Anil was not accusing Ted of being a liar, but rather trying to understand why Franco had not shown up when Ted had said he would. By shifting the conversation to the question of whether or not Ted is a liar, Ted avoids facing Anil's real question. Third, Ted's accusation escalates the conflict. Anil hadn't intended to call Ted a liar, so by using a strong word like *liar* himself, Ted challenges Anil either to accuse him of something quite serious or to leave him alone entirely.

159. Albert assumes the energy sent to the heating element will be at least equal to the energy needed to boil the water. This isn't true. Among other things, some of the initial energy is dissipated as heat by the friction used to generate the electrical energy. For centuries, people have tried to invent perpetual motion machines similar to Albert's, but none have yet succeeded.

160. The second glass. Doubling the radius of the base doubles the glass's size in two dimensions (depth and width) while doubling the height doubles the glass's size in only one dimension (height). In fact, the second glass will have twice the volume of the first glass.

161. He must take the chicken across, come back, take the grain across, take the chicken back, take the fox across, go back, and then take the chicken across.

162. Put the backpack on, step on the scale, and see how much you and the pack weigh together. Then take off the pack and weigh yourself again. The difference between the two readings will give you the weight of the pack.

163. It takes three moves to get to d5, two moves to get to a3, four moves to get to b6, and three moves to get to g4.

164. A base-eight counting system, also known as an octal system. (Since the decimal system is often represented by the three letters *dec*, and the octal system is often represented by the three letters *oct*, you could say that *dec*[25] and *oct*[31] are equal.

165. It would only be true if nobody loved anybody. If anybody loves somebody, then everybody loves that person. That would mean that everybody loves somebody, which in turn would mean that everybody loves everybody.

166. It would connect to the middle of the three line segments. The fact that it seems to connect with the leftmost line segment is due to an optical illusion.

167. Twenty-seven. Sixteen small triangles, seven triangles containing four small triangles (don't forget the one that's upside down), three triangles containing nine small triangles, and then the one big triangle.

168. You would want the chain to wrap around the smaller of the two gears connected to the pedals and the larger of the two gears connected to the back wheel. Pedaling takes less effort the less the back wheel moves with each rotation of the pedals. After one rotation of the pedals, the chain will have moved a distance equal to the circumference of the gear connected to the pedals. Therefore, the chain will have moved a shorter distance if the circumference of the gear connected to the pedals is smaller. The back wheel will make a full rotation in the same amount of time as it takes the back wheel's gear to make a full rotation. The larger the gear attached to the back wheel, the greater distance the bicycle chain will have to move in order to make a full rotation. Therefore, the back wheel will move more slowly and with greater effort if the gear attached to it is larger.

169. Arrange the six matches to form a three-sided pyramid (tetrahedron) with a triangular base.

170. She should put the gun against her head right away and pull the trigger. Since two out of the six chambers are loaded, spinning the barrel gives her a one in three chance of winding up with a bullet in her head. On the other hand, since the two chambers with bullets are adjacent, she knows that only one of the four empty chambers will click over to a chamber with a bullet in it once it has failed to fire. So there is only a one in four chance of firing a bullet if she doesn't spin the barrel.

171. Answers may vary. One solution is to lead the elephant onto a boat standing in water and then draw a line on the boat's hull marking how far the water reaches when the elephant's on board. Then lead the elephant off the boat and add known quantities of weights to the boat until the boat sinks down to the line you drew. You then know the elephant weighs the same amount as the weights you added to the boat.

172. Because she has told a phony story. Frost forms on the inside of glass, not the outside.

173. Ten coins. You would need four pennies, one nickel, two dimes, and three quarters.

174. She can offer $1 to her third-in-command, nothing to her second-in-command, and keep all the rest of the money for herself. The only way she will be killed is if both thieves vote against her. If she is killed, the second-in-command can then take all the money for himself because the lowly third-in-command won't have enough voting power to go against him. So the third-in-command will reason that the $1 she is being offered by the leader is preferable to the nothing she would be offered if she voted to kill the leader. The third-in-command will not vote to kill the leader, and the leader can live happily with her $999,999.

175. The North and South Poles. Every direction from the North Pole is south and every direction from the South Pole is north. The sun only rises and sets once a year at the poles, but when it does so, it rises in the south if you're at the North Pole and it rises in the north if you're at the South Pole.

176. Since she was working the midnight shift, she knew that in exactly one week the sun would not shine—because it would be night.

177. The solution is sketched below.

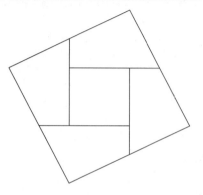

178. This claim is itself based neither on what we see, hear, smell, taste, or touch nor on a process of logical deduction. Therefore, according to its own argument, this claim is strictly meaningless.

179. Ten. Lockers numbered 1, 4, 9, 16, 25, 36, 49, 64, 81, and 100—in other words, all the square numbers between one and one hundred, inclusive. Though a little trial and error is probably the easiest way to solve this problem, there is also a mathematical explanation. Any locker with a number that is a factor of any other locker number will be toggled. For instance, locker 12 will be toggled when students are toggling at locker 1, locker 2, locker 3, locker 4, and locker 6. Every number that isn't square will have an even number of factors: $12 = 1 \times 12 = 2 \times 6 = 3 \times 4$. That means that every locker that doesn't have a square number will be shut just as many times as it is opened. Because one of the factors of a square number multiplies by itself to produce the square, square numbers have an odd number of factors: $36 = 1 \times 36 = 2 \times 18 = 3 \times 12 = 4 \times 9 = 6 \times 6$. Locker 36 will be toggled with lockers 1, 2, 3, 4, 6, 9, 12, 18, and itself, locker 36, for a total of nine toggles, meaning that it will be opened one more time than it is closed.

180. Fold the sheet of paper over so that the image of the pig falls on top of the image of the pigpen.